56 Azuela: Los de abajo

Critical Guides to Spanish Texts

EDITED BY J.E. VAREY, A.D. DEYERMOND AND C. DAVIES

AZUELA

Los de abajo

Clive Griffin

Fellow and Tutor in Spanish, Trinity College, Oxford
Lecturer in Latin-American Literature, University of Oxford

Grant & Cutler Ltd
in association with Tamesis Books Ltd

ISBN 0 7293 0336 5

I.S.B.N. 84-599-3306-7

DEPÓSITO LEGAL: V. 216-1993

Printed in Spain by
Artes Gráficas Soler, S.A., Valencia
for
GRANT & CUTLER LTD
55-57 GREAT MARLBOROUGH STREET, LONDON WIV 2AY

Contents

*For Don Dummer and Stuart Philp
in gratitude*

Prefatory Note

The edition referred to in this study is Mariano Azuela, *Los de abajo*, edited by W.A.R. Richardson (London: Harrap, 1973 and subsequent reprints). Details of earlier editions are to be found below, on pp.25-27. Page references to the novel are indicated thus: (150). The figures in parentheses in italic type refer to the numbered items in the Bibliographical Note, where necessary followed by volume and page numbers, thus: (*5*, II, p.22).

I wish to thank the Interfaculty Committee for Latin-American Studies of the University of Oxford for a travel grant which enabled me to carry out preliminary research for this study in Mexico; the Humanities Research Centre of the Australian National University, Canberra, for appointing me to a Visiting Fellowship during which time I prepared most of the first draft; my friends at the HRC for their kindness and help during that blissful period; my colleagues John Rutherford and Laurence Whitehead for their advice; Alan Deyermond and John Varey for their careful editing of my manuscript; and, as ever, my brother, Nigel Griffin. The mistakes and stupidities which remain despite the generous help I have received are, of course, all my own.

1. Azuela and the Mexican Revolution

Mariano Azuela (1873-1952) wrote and published the first version of *Los de abajo*, his best-known work and the most important novel of the Mexican Revolution, in 1915 during the armed phase of the upheaval. The novel is largely a personal recreation and interpretation of real situations, many of which Azuela heard about first-hand from participants or witnessed himself. It is the only one of his works set during the Revolution to deal with revolutionary peasants but, like the others, it presents a strikingly faithful picture of what it was like for many Mexicans to live through that turbulent period. It is therefore important in any study of *Los de abajo* to examine, albeit briefly, the history of the Revolution and Azuela's own experience of it.

The Mexican Revolution (1910-1917)

No simple explanation for the outbreak and subsequent development of the Revolution is convincing. Some historians have depicted it as a straightforward struggle between social classes, and literary critics influenced by this view have attempted to explain Azuela's portrayal of the Revolution and his attitude to it by reference to his middle-class origin; this, according to such critics, led him to distort or misunderstand the Revolution, some commentators even claiming that the novel is ideologically reactionary despite its esthetic innovations. Not only are such judgements questionable, but recent historical research has demonstrated that no simplistic class analysis of the Revolution is sustainable. Indeed, the Mexican Revolution has proved particularly resistant to explanations based upon rigid *a priori* assumptions and resulting in convenient generalizations. One reason for this is that, rather than a coherent struggle between social classes or ideologies, it was a complex and frequently confused network of separate revolts which, while they coalesced to form a national revolution, had different causes and took different forms in the various regions of Mexico. Although some revolutionaries clearly resented the middle and upper classes (the 'curros' and 'catrines' to whom the characters of *Los de abajo* constantly refer), no political party or group of intellectuals succeeded in imposing an ideology on the participants of the armed phase of the Revolution. With the exception of Emiliano Zapata who led a struggle for agrarian reform in the small but strategic state of Morelos[1] in which traditional rural life had been disrupted by new agricultural practices, few of the revolutionaries had anything approaching a defined programme. They merely responded in an *ad hoc* fashion to rapidly shifting events. Although popular rural discontent was at the root of many of the revolts, vague aspirations, personal grievances and ambitions, or merely a thirst for loot dominated a chaotic, bloody, and often aimless struggle which gradually acquired its own momentum. The armed phase of the Revolution petered out after 1917 because, as much as anything, the country and its people were exhausted by the slaughter and devastation wreaked by countless military campaigns: it has been estimated that between 1910 and 1921 one in every fourteen Mexicans had been killed in the fighting or had died as a result of the epidemics and starvation associated with it. The complexity and frequent incoherence of the Revolution means that the following summary can be no more than a sketch.

President Porfirio Díaz had ruled the country in person or by proxy and in an authoritarian manner since 1876, bringing political stability and economic development to Mexico. These achievements had been at the expense both of the relative autonomy previously enjoyed by local centres and regions, and of rural and urban workers who were exploited by powerful landowners (*hacendados*) and by foreign capitalists whose investment Díaz had attracted to Mexico. The result was an explosive mixture of rapacious capitalist development, bitter resentment of central authority, and a virtually pre-

---

[1]For maps giving the location of towns and states in Mexico, see *3*, pp.198-201.

market society in much of the countryside (where eighty-five per cent. of Mexico's population lived). Díaz's great achievement, the introduction of the railways, had fuelled economic growth, but had worsened the peasants' plight: rail transport opened up new markets, allowing *hacendados* to cultivate profitable cash crops for export from their regions rather than producing the traditional foodstuffs consumed by the local peasantry. The cultivation of cash crops also encouraged *hacendados* to appropriate more land from food-producing smallholders. Dispossessed smallholders (*rancheros*) understandably resented local landowners and bosses (*caciques*) — such as Don Mónico in Azuela's novel — who owed their power to Díaz's regime. In addition, there was in the years immediately preceding the Revolution a major economic downswing in Mexico, largely owing to the depression of the American economy. In 1908 and 1909 the predicament of the poor was further exacerbated by disastrous harvests. All of this led to a crippling rise in the price the peasants had to pay for their staple foodstuffs, and it was accompanied by growing rural unemployment. The scene was thus set for unrest both in the agrarian regions where the need for land reform was keenly felt (e.g. Morelos) and in the isolated communities of the *sierras* which had recently seen their local autonomy eroded by Porfirian centralism and which were facing increased fiscal burdens. But discontent was not limited to the countryside. In the country the powder was dry; but the fuse was lit in the cities.

Díaz's centralism operated at both national and local levels, and was based on a network consisting of *caciques*, powerful civilians who owed allegiance to him, and of his local political executive (the *jefes políticos*). Middle-class liberals, themselves a product of Díaz's economic development, were impatient to wrest a share of political power from his oligarchy; at the same time, they were concerned by his reluctance to institutionalize his regime. In 1910 he was eighty years of age, his career was clearly nearing its end, and the stability which had fostered the development of a middle class would be undermined if there were to be a vacuum left after his death. Although Díaz had created the conditions in which a middle class could flourish, he now appeared to it to be a liability.

In 1908 he had given a misleading but widely publicized newspaper interview in which he had made the surprising claim that he would welcome democratic opposition to his government. He also said that he would not run again for the presidency. In the same year Francisco I. Madero, a wealthy, well intentioned, but somewhat ingenuous liberal, published a book in which he discussed the presidential election that was due to take place in 1910, condemning in advance any attempt by Díaz to have himself re-elected. Madero's subsequent campaign against Díaz's re-election gained wide support from liberals; in addition, many opportunists jumped on the *maderista* bandwagon, believing that it offered them a chance of political power. Faced for the first time by a broad opposition, Díaz had Madero imprisoned, increasing popular support for him. When, after fraudulent elections, Díaz was declared President for yet another term of office, Madero fled to the United States whence he called for an armed insurrection to take place on 20 November 1910 to remove the dictator.

Madero's aims were limited and his expectations naïve. He had no clear social programme and, apart from a desire for justice and moral regeneration, his main objective was political reform which would result in a free vote and prevent the re-election of Díaz. He imagined that his call to arms would provoke a rapid and limited urban revolt to topple the aged dictator and his morally bankrupt gerontocracy. The response to the call was, however, slow and sporadic for, when Díaz was declared President, many *maderistas* lost interest in their cause and carried on living and working as before. However, when Mexicans learnt of the Federal Army's inability to scotch isolated outbreaks of *maderista* insurrection, support for Madero grew. Díaz manipulated a tame press in an attempt to convince Mexicans that his army (*los federales*) was putting down the rising, but his propaganda was so transparently false that it served only to provoke resentment against the regime and to increase Madero's popularity. While government and army were busy revealing their failure to deal with a feeble insurrection, the rebels (flying the colours of *maderismo* but in reality a loose alliance of disparate factions and local interests) won growing popular support and gained military momentum, especially in the north of the country. After a series of skirmishes, the rebels, led by Pancho Villa and Pascual Orozco, eventually won a success in May 1911 with the capture of Ciudad Juárez on the United States border. Although this was far from being a devastating military reverse for Díaz, his response was that of an old man who no longer had the stomach for a fight: he negotiated with his opponents and agreed to go into exile.

Having achieved his modest aim of removing Díaz, Madero called for the disbandment of the rebel troops, leaving the *porfirista* power structure and the Federal Army intact — in *Los de abajo* Luis Cervantes parodies Madero's instructions to the rebels: 'Amigos, muchas gracias; ahora vuélvanse a sus casas' (107). However, an irresistible force had by now been unleashed: the rural revolutionaries whom Azuela would later portray in his novel. In the event, Madero was to have as much trouble from a popular peasant leader like Zapata, whose goal was agrarian reform, or from a *caudillo* like Villa, as he did from Díaz's reactionary old guard.

With Díaz's exile, the internal contradictions of *maderismo* became apparent: some supporters wanted a thoroughgoing social revolution; some desired limited reform; and yet others, described by Azuela in his memoirs (5, III, pp.1068-71) and in his bitter novel *Andrés Pérez, maderista*, were erstwhile *porfiristas* who cynically adopted the outward trappings of *maderismo* for their own ends. By the time he was elected President of Mexico in October 1911, Madero's conciliatory attitude to the old regime had cost him much of his initial support. Believing that Madero was not going to implement radical changes, Zapata published in November 1911 a revolutionary manifesto for land reform — the Plan de Ayala — and refused to lay down his arms. Zapata's assumptions were correct, an indication of Madero's policies being his inclusion in his cabinet of Venustiano Carranza, a rich and ambitious conservative who had been a senator under Díaz. Carranza was subsequently to become a key figure in the Revolution.

The period of Madero's government was punctuated by crises. During one of several revolts, his former supporter Orozco defeated government troops, and Madero responded by taking the disastrous decision to appoint an arch-conservative officer, Victoriano Huerta, to high military command. In early 1913 the old dictator's nephew, Félix Díaz, and General Bernardo Reyes, both of whom had been imprisoned for leading armed revolts against Madero but had been imprudently shown clemency by him, conspired once again to overthrow the President. This time they were successful. Díaz and Reyes were released from prison by the disaffected Federal Army, and the Ciudadela (Mexico City's old arsenal) was captured and fortified. The loyal guard of the National Palace resisted, but during ten days of fighting in February between the Ciudadela and the Palace — the *Decena trágica* — it became clear that Huerta, whom Madero had unwisely put in charge of his defence despite warnings of his complicity with the rebels, was indeed in league with Félix Díaz. Madero was captured with the blessing of the American ambassador, and shortly afterwards Huerta had Madero and his Vice-President murdered.

Huerta emerged as the new ruler of Mexico. He gained conservative support including that of many of the old *caciques* who had passed themselves off as *maderistas*, and that of a large proportion of the middle class which had been shocked by the violence of revolutionaries such as Zapata. Huerta's authoritarian but incompetent military regime attempted to turn the clock back to the days of Díaz and establish a dictatorship supported by the army, the Church and the aristocracy. However, Madero's murder and Huerta's usurpation of power provoked the rising of armed bands in the countryside, and Carranza, whose struggle against Huerta was motivated by personal ambition rather than by any reformist ideals, attempted to harness this Revolution to his own ends. In March 1913 he declared himself the leader of the armed *constitucionalista*[2] opposition to Huerta and gathered together a large fighting force in the north of the country under the command of Villa, Pablo González, and his own loyal supporter, Alvaro Obregón. Huerta,

---

[2]This term originally denoted the armed opposition to Huerta. Later, with the split between Carranza and Villa, it came to be used to refer to the former's faction, Villa's supporters being known as *convencionistas*.

who was almost permanently drunk, was inept and ignorant, and his conscript army weak and disloyal. The resounding defeat of the *federales* came in June 1914 when Villa and Pánfilo Natera captured the town of Zacatecas. Three weeks later Huerta fled into exile, and the Federal Army surrendered.

As had happened with the departure of Díaz three years earlier, the temporary unity of the revolutionaries dissolved once the common enemy had been defeated. It had long been clear that Villa and Carranza mistrusted each other and, indeed, after his victory at Zacatecas, Villa did not immediately advance on Mexico City because he feared *carrancista* incursions into the north of the country where he had his power-base. Obregón was thus able to occupy the capital in August 1914, and Carranza began to issue dictatorial decrees from Mexico City as soon as he, in turn, arrived there. Opposition between Villa and Carranza was inevitable: Villa was a violent, capricious and impulsive military *caudillo* whose personalist regime was one of social banditry, and whose forces and allies were predominantly motivated by local considerations. Carranza for his part was outwardly respectable and legalistically minded, his followers had a somewhat more national perspective, he had promised a return to civilian government after the triumph of the Revolution, and he wanted as little change as possible from the days of Porfirio Díaz. Thus began the bloodiest phase of the Revolution.

In an attempt to heal the split a convention was called for October 1914 in the town of Aguascalientes, but it only brought to a head the differences between the two factions. Villa, with the support of the *zapatistas*, declared Carranza and his *constitu-cionalista* allies to be in revolt against the *convencionista* government (taking its name from the Convención de Aguascalientes) which Villa and Zapata supported and controlled. The *zapatistas* thus joined the mainstream of the Revolution but were to prove unreliable allies because they were almost exclusively concerned with their native state of Morelos, and had a poor record of fighting outside it. Obregón, for his part, sided with Carranza and took command of the *constitucionalista* forces. These he withdrew to Veracruz where Carranza consolidated and, uncharacteristically but successfully, set about winning the support of the peasantry and workers by proclaiming a reformist programme. *Villistas* and *zapatistas* occupied the centre of the country and Mexico City itself where their behaviour — innocently uncouth or plain barbaric — horrified the urban inhabitants. The *constitucionalistas* and the *convencionistas* occupied the city by turns, reducing it to chaos and bankruptcy until, after three months of inconclusive fighting between the two opposing forces, Villa unwisely decided to attack Obregón's army. The series of battles which took place at Celaya in April 1915, at León in May and June, and at Aguascalientes in July proved the turning point of the Revolution. Although outnumbered by Villa's forces, Obregón was well supplied and, having learnt from the experiences of the great armies then at war in Europe, was tactically more sophisticated than the militarily primitive *villistas*. Villa was defeated and obliged to retreat north until, in December 1915, he lost even his northern power-base of Chihuahua; Zapata went south to his native Morelos. In the following year Carranza consolidated his victory over the *convencionistas*, taking control of almost all the country. Villa was forced into guerrilla activity in the north while the *zapatista* revolution returned to what at heart it had always been: a local phenomenon.

In late 1916 Carranza called a convention at Querétaro to rubber-stamp a conservative constitution which went back on the vague reformist promises he had made earlier. However, many of the *constitucionalistas*, headed by Obregón, forced him to accept the more radical and intensely nationalistic constitution of 1917 which paved the way for the sort of reforms which were later to be implemented in Mexico and which were to shape the way the country's political and social structure would develop under successive governments. The Querétaro Convention and the 1917 Constitution brought to an end the armed phase of a revolution which had shaken Mexico from top to bottom and which has obsessed Mexicans ever since.

Azuela, the Revolution in Jalisco, and 'Los de abajo'

Azuela's experiences of the Revolution were largely confined to Jalisco, Aguascalientes and Zacatecas where most of the action of *Los de abajo* takes place. These three states lie west and north-west of Mexico City. They contain, in the east of Jalisco, Azuela's birthplace, Lagos de Moreno; Guadalajara, then the second city of Mexico, located at the centre of the same state; the towns of Aguascalientes and Zacatecas themselves; and smaller towns and villages which the author knew and introduced into the novel. His personal involvement in the armed phase of the Revolution spanned a nine-month period from the end of October 1914 to July 1915, and he set *Los de abajo* in those same years. It probably begins in about April 1914[3] with Demetrio Macías, the central character of the novel, and his band fighting Huerta's Federal troops; they subsequently take part in the attack on Zacatecas, throw in their lot with the *villistas* after the Aguascalientes Convention and, presumably in the month of June 1915, are wiped out in a confrontation with the victorious *carrancistas*.

Azuela had spent most of his life in Jalisco and considered himself a minor provincial writer (5, III, pp.1012, 1125); indeed, Mexican critics may well have ignored or been unaware of *Los de abajo* because its author lived, worked and published in the provinces at a time when the country's cultural life was firmly centred upon Mexico City (4, p.186). His father was a shopkeeper and after beginning his schooling at Lagos, Azuela went to Guadalajara, the capital of the state of Jalisco, completed his secondary education, and then spent eight years studying medicine there. In 1899 he returned to Lagos where he set up as a general practitioner. As a student he had read widely, especially nineteenth-century French and Spanish novels; European realism was, as we shall see in Chapters 2 and 3, to have a lasting influence on his own works. He had composed one novel during this period, and he continued to write while working as a doctor.

---

[3]Many critics maintain that the action begins in mid 1913. This is a possible interpretation (see below, p.100).

In the course of his childhood, training, and medical practice, he had — so he later assures us — come to sympathize with the poorer elements of Mexican society, particularly with the *rancheros* of Jalisco. Although he was later to paint a somewhat ambiguous picture of life under the rule of Porfirio Díaz, comparing it favourably with the corruption of post-revolutionary Mexico (5, III, p.1066), Azuela was a liberal, an opponent of Díaz's re-election in 1910, and a supporter of Madero. His subsequent explanation that *maderismo* was attractive to him because of his thirst for adventure to relieve the tedium of life during Díaz's regime seems, at best, to be only partial (5, III, p.1067). He and his friend, the poet José Becerra, were the leading *maderistas* in Lagos, their political activities provoking the animosity of the local *caciques*. After the declaration of Díaz's re-election in 1910 Azuela organized *maderista* opposition in Lagos but, despite sporadic armed risings against the dictator in other parts of Jalisco, Lagos was untouched by violence, and his involvement was purely political. With Díaz's fall in 1911, Azuela put up as a *maderista* candidate for the post of *jefe político* for Lagos and won a large majority. It is not surprising, given Azuela's support of Madero, that *Los de abajo* depicts at least six of the perceived evils which *maderista* programmes sought to eradicate: *caciquismo*, the ignorance of the masses, alcoholism, gambling, prostitution and bloodsports. Azuela's election appeared to be a triumph for liberal idealism. Many years later he was to criticize Madero for his ingenuous optimism and for failing to build a popular base for his movement, but he does not seem to have appreciated how unrealistically limited were Madero's aims (5, III, pp.1072-73). What he did soon realize was that opportunists were taking over the *maderista* revolution; he was himself a victim of the *caciques*, and the old guard of Porfirianism now masquerading as *maderistas* did everything in its power to frustrate his efforts as *jefe político*. When, after some two months in the post, Azuela saw a political intriguer become Governor of Jalisco, he resigned and returned to his medical practice. To add insult to injury, he was obliged to hand over his office to the very *cacique* who had attempted to prevent him from assuming his post as *jefe político* in the first place. For Azuela this was a moment of utter disillusionment with the *maderista* revolution (5, III, p.1070). The hijacking of the Revolution by self-seekers was to become a constant theme in his cycle of novels set during the revolutionary period, the first of which was his acerbic *Andrés Pérez, maderista*, one of the only two novels of the Mexican Revolution to be published as early as 1911. The picture of the Revolution which emerged from that work, and more particularly from *Los de abajo*, would, in time, come to exercise a profound influence upon the development of the twentieth-century Mexican novel.

Jalisco had remained on the margin of Madero's revolution but, with his assassination, there was considerable opposition to the *federales* in the west of the state. However, the revolutionary bands tended, like that of Demetrio Macías, to be uncoordinated and isolated from the mainstream of the *constitucionalista* military campaigns. Lagos itself was again spared any violence at this time. The most important revolutionary leader in Jalisco was an ex-black-smith, Julián Medina, who, when he became aware of the existence of Obregón's *constitucionalista* army, joined forces with it for the advance on Guadalajara. The city was occupied by the *constitucionalistas* on 8 July 1914, two weeks after the defeat of the *federales* at Zacatecas.

Meanwhile, at Lagos, Azuela had withdrawn from political activity after his resignation from the post of *jefe político*. After Madero's death, genuine *maderistas* were persecuted by Huerta's supporters in Jalisco, but the repression at Lagos had not been harsh and Azuela was in no immediate danger. He spent the period of the Madero and Huerta governments working as a doctor and writing, but he knew that he was under surveillance and was careful to hide the manuscript of his virulent attack on *caciquismo*, the novel *Los caciques* (not published until 1917), in case its discovery by his political enemies compromised him. He was finishing the final chapter of this work when news of Villa's victory at Zacatecas reached Lagos with the retreating *federales*. Although he was not involved at this stage with the *villista* forces, it would not be long before Azuela heard accounts of the battle for Zacatecas from those

who had been members of the victorious army. He would draw upon
these accounts in *Los de abajo*.

With the flight of Huerta it seemed to Azuela that the
Revolution had at last triumphed, but he was soon undeceived and
was obliged to take an active part in the most bloody phase of the
fighting — that period to which he refers in his memoirs, employing
a vocabulary familiar to the reader of *Los de abajo*, as the 'tormenta',
'ventarrón', and 'huracán' (5, III, pp.1078, 1085, 1095) of the rivalry
between Villa and Carranza. He remained in the backwater of Lagos
de Moreno during the summer of 1914 while Villa and Carranza
were gradually drawing apart after their temporary co-operation in
the defeat of Huerta. In September, Villa declared that he no longer
recognized Carranza's authority as leader of the Revolution, and in
October the Aguascalientes Convention was called, as we have seen,
in an attempt to reconcile the two factions. Although Julián Medina
had fought alongside Obregón's *constitucionalistas* in the capture of
Guadalajara, at the Convention he threw in his lot with Villa and the
convencionista government. As the two factions proceeded to
occupy various regions of the country in preparation for war, Medina
was appointed Governor of the State of Jalisco which was largely
villista although the *carrancistas* still had to be ousted from
Guadalajara. In late October 1914, on his way through Lagos after
the Aguascalientes Convention, one of Medina's officers recruited
Azuela.

It is, perhaps, strange that such a solitary and introspective
man as Azuela should, in middle age, have abandoned his determination to remain on the sidelines of the Revolution after the
decline of *maderismo*. Nevertheless, several factors seem to have
influenced his decision: his friendship with José Becerra who was
already a member of Medina's forces and who was instrumental in
the attempt to recruit him; his awareness that he might fall victim to
his political enemies in Lagos who would be quick to exploit
factional confusion to settle old scores; his belief that the *convencionistas* represented the legal government of Mexico; and a disdain
for elitist intellectuals who sheltered in their ivory towers while
events of national importance were taking place (27, pp.174-75). He

may even have had an artistic motive for enlisting: he was later to claim that he had welcomed the chance of close contact with common revolutionaries because such an experience would provide him with the raw material for a book. Although this may appear an odd reason to risk his skin with a band of fighters whom he did not hesitate to describe as ignorant and brutal thugs, it is not entirely implausible: as a writer, Azuela was a convinced realist with several novels already to his name, and he advocated the virtues for the novelist of the close observation of potential subject-matter.

Whatever his motives, he found himself involved in the armed Revolution, with the rank of lieutenant-colonel and a post on Medina's general staff as head of medical services. By throwing in his lot with Medina, he found himself caught up particularly with the *villista* faction of the *convencionistas*.

Azuela joined up at Irapuato, a railway junction south-east of Lagos (the railways were of great importance in the Mexican Revolution, a fact reflected in the numerous scenes of rail travel found in the novels of the Revolution, including *Los de abajo*). Here Medina was obliged to wait for six weeks for *convencionista* reinforcements to arrive from Mexico City before an attack on Guadalajara could be launched. During that period of enforced inactivity Azuela lived with Medina and his followers, and had ample opportunity to indulge his predilection for observation. He tells us that some of the *rancheros* who made up Medina's forces were idealists, but most were moved by hatred of their local *cacique*, by the thirst for personal revenge, or by the desire for adventure — motives which are reflected in the members of Macías's band in *Los de abajo*. Azuela seems to have admired Medina himself, but contact with the mass of his comrades was depressing in the extreme:

> Muy pronto la primitiva y favorable impresión que tenía [yo] de sus hombres se fue desvaneciendo en un cuadro de sombrío desencanto y pesar. El espíritu de amor y sacrificio que alentara con tanto fervor como poca esperanza en el triunfo a los primeros revolucionarios, había desaparecido. Las manifestaciones exteriores que

me dieron los actuales dueños de la situación, lo que ante
mis ojos se presentó, fue un mundillo de amistades
fingidas, envidias, adulación, espionaje, intrigas,
chismes y perfidias. Nadie pensaba ya sino en la mejor
tajada del pastel a la vista. [...] Mi situación fue entonces
la de Solís en mi novela. '¿Por qué — le pregunta el
seudorrevolucionario y logrero Luis Cervantes — si está
desencantado de la revolución, sigue en ella?' 'Porque la
revolución — responde Solís — es el huracán, y el
hombre que se entrega a ella no es ya el hombre, sino la
miserable hoja seca arrebatada por el vendaval.' (5, III,
pp.1080-81)

Eventually, in mid-December, Villa arrived at Irapuato; his troops
were transported towards Guadalajara by train, and the outnumbered
carrancistas prudently retreated to the south-west of Jalisco,
abandoning the city and allowing Villa to make a triumphal entry on
17 December 1914 virtually unopposed. Medina, now properly
installed in the state capital, appointed Azuela to the post of Director
of Public Education for Jalisco. Azuela thus became a bureaucrat in
the service of the *villistas*, though he was soon involved in the war of
attrition that characterized the later stages of the Revolution. Just as
Mexico City itself was alternately occupied by *convencionistas* and
constitucionalistas, so Guadalajara changed hands several times. In
mid-January 1915, only four weeks after having retreated from
Guadalajara, the reinforced *carrancistas* had regrouped and were
back outside the city. After fierce fighting, Medina's forces were
obliged to flee, and it appears that Azuela escaped the city in the
nick of time, for the *carrancistas* were not kindly disposed towards
those who had co-operated with Medina. In mid-February 1915, the
villistas returned to the offensive: the *carrancistas* again abandoned
Guadalajara, Villa made a second entry into the city to be greeted
once again by jubilant crowds, and Medina and Azuela resumed
their offices. This was the peak of *villista* fortunes in Jalisco; barely
two months later Villa's defeat at Celaya was to mark the beginning
of the end for the *convencionistas*.

The effect on Jalisco of that defeat was immediate. It was clear that for strategic reasons Guadalajara could no longer be held, and on 16 and 17 April the soldiers, accompanied by the bureaucrats who had worked with the *villistas*, fled the city by train for Lagos; Azuela escaped as the doctor in charge of the train's hospital coach; and on 18 April the *carrancistas* were once again in control of Guadalajara. For six weeks Medina and Azuela remained at Lagos which was situated in a staunchly *villista* area, but in June the *carrancistas'* advance obliged Medina to pull out of the town. Lagos was no longer safe for Azuela, and he was again forced to leave his home with Medina. As was the case with the majority of participants in the Revolution, Medina was motivated by essentially local concerns: when the *villistas* were driven out of the major towns of Jalisco, Villa asked Medina to go north with him, but it appears that Medina refused, determining instead to remain in his home state and to wrest Guadalajara once more from the *carrancistas*.

Azuela had been observing the revolutionaries, making notes for *Los de abajo* for several months, and had even written, or at least sketched out, some chapters in Guadalajara. However, the most important period for the gestation of *Los de abajo* was that which followed Medina's abortive attack on that city (15 June 1915). As medical officer for Medina's forces, Azuela had been left in Tepatitlán, some 50 kms east of Guadalajara, to await casualties from the attack. One such proved to be Manuel Caloca, a young colonel whom Azuela liked and admired. It was clear to him that Caloca required an operation and that this could not be performed in Tepatitlán. He therefore undertook a long journey by horse to accompany the wounded officer and a band of his followers to Aguascalientes whither the bulk of Villa's forces had withdrawn after their defeats at Celaya and León. The journey lasted just over three weeks (approximately from 17 June until 10 July). It was particularly hazardous because the *carrancistas* held the direct route from Tepatitlán to Aguascalientes; Caloca and his band were thus obliged to follow a circuitous course, much of it over difficult terrain, and were frequently in danger of attack from *carrancistas* and the roving groups of bandits which infested the states of Jalisco

and Zacatecas at this time. The route took them from Tepatitlán
through Cuquío, Limón, the Juchipila canyon, Santa Rosa, Moyahua,
Juchipila itself, Jalpa, and Calvillo to Aguascalientes. The reader of
Los de abajo will recognize the itinerary as that taken by Demetrio
Macías; indeed, Azuela was to base a good deal of the novel on what
he witnessed in the course of this journey during which he had direct
experience of combat, probably for the first time. Although he said
that he had originally thought of basing the character of Macías upon
Julián Medina, he later used Caloca as a model for certain aspects of
Demetrio (and Caloca did, indeed, recognize himself in this character). Azuela made copious notes for his novel during the journey —
he chose to locate Demetrio's smallholding in Limón and Don
Mónico's home in Moyahua — and it is no coincidence that he
makes Macías's band return to Juchipila in precisely the same month
as he and the wounded Caloca passed through the town (*28*, p.63).
Other details such as the desertion by *villista* soldiers (Azuela and
Caloca left Tepatitlán with eighty men, arriving at Aguascalientes
with only fourteen) and the poverty and hunger he describes in the
ravaged villages of the Juchipila area are taken directly from his
observations in the months of June and July 1915.

Azuela and Caloca arrived in Aguascalientes just in time, for it
was already under attack by Obregón's forces. Azuela immediately
operated on Caloca and, the same day, accompanied his patient on
one of the last *villista* trains to leave the city before it fell to the
constitucionalistas. He delivered Caloca to the *villista* military
hospital in Chihuahua and there, during the months of August,
September and October, set about writing up *Los de abajo* from his
notes. In October, with most of the novel written, he left for the
border town of Ciudad Juárez in search of a publisher. He was to
find one just across the United States frontier in El Paso where he
hastily completed it. *Los de abajo* immediately appeared in serial
form.

On 20 December Ciudad Juárez surrendered to the *carrancistas*, and Azuela took advantage of the ensuing confusion to slip back
into Mexico and take a train to Guadalajara where he had left his
family. He soon decided to settle in Mexico City and there built up a

modest medical practice in a poor quarter. He was to continue to
write in his spare time, his disillusionment with the Revolution —
and especially with the corruption of Carranza's government —
being evident in the remaining novels of his cycle dealing with the
Revolution (*Las moscas*, *Domitilo quiere ser diputado*, and *Las
tribulaciones de una familia decente* — all published in 1918).
Meanwhile, he made substantial revisions to *Los de abajo* which
appeared in a new version in 1920.

* * * * *

The text used by Richardson for his edition of *Los de abajo* comes
from the definitive version published in 1958 (*5*, I, pp.320-418).
This, like the numerous editions which appeared after the rediscov-
ery of the neglected novel by Mexican critics in 1924 and 1925,
ultimately derives — with only a few subsequent emendations by the
author — from the one printed at Azuela's own expense by
Tipografía Razaster in Mexico City in 1920. The original version of
Los de abajo, first published in twenty-three instalments in the El
Paso (Texas) newspaper *El Paso del Norte* from 27 October to 21
November 1915 (and reprinted in book form at El Paso in December
1915[4], as a serial in the Tampico (Tamaulipas, Mexico) daily
newspaper *El Mundo* in 1917, and in book form at Tampico in the
same year), was substantially modified by Azuela for the 1920
edition.

The first version had been hastily written. Azuela had drafted
some of it while on the run from the victorious *carrancista* forces,
and he improvised Part Three in the offices of *El Paso del Norte* to
which he had sold the novel because he was desperately short of
money. He had little time to revise the manuscript which was rushed
into print as soon as he had completed it. Even the few well-disposed
critics who praised *Los de abajo* when it first appeared in 1915
hinted that it needed polishing (*28*, pp.95-97), and Azuela himself

---

[4]Almost all critics record the date of this edition as 1916 which is, indeed,
the year printed on its title-page. However, Robe's thorough bibliographical
research shows that it really appeared in 1915 (*28*, p.93).

was clearly dissatisfied with the original version. He also became increasingly disillusioned between 1915 and 1920 with the way the Revolution had developed under the rule of Carranza. His desire to improve his novel and his growing disillusion with Mexican politics are apparent from the changes he made.

Stanley Robe's publication of the first version (*28*, pp.123-67) enables a comparison to be made between the El Paso editions and the modified version of 1920. The most important of the many changes made by Azuela are as follows:

He increased the length of the novel by approximately one fifth. In particular, Chapter 1 of Part Three is expanded, and two new chapters (2 and 3) are interpolated into the same Part. The major effect of these additions concerns the characters of Valderrama and Cervantes, Valderrama being an afterthought who fits unhappily into the later version of the novel: he is a completely new character modelled upon Azuela's close friend José Becerra. The interpolated chapters introduce Valderrama, refer to Villa's defeat at Celaya, more generally emphasize the decline of *villismo* (references to Villa are accordingly toned down or, on occasion, cut out altogether), emphasize the disillusion of Macías's band, and contrast the hostile reception given to the revolutionaries on their return to Juchipila with the reaction of the local inhabitants when Macías first visited them. Writing in 1920 with the benefit of hindsight, Azuela stresses the inevitability of the *convencionistas'* decline. Most of Chapter 6 of Part One is also new: it makes Cervantes more obviously cynical, greedy, cowardly and mendacious. Other less important additions to the novel serve the same end and also emphasize the author's pessimism.

These changes, together with different chapter divisions, provide the novel with a more balanced structure. Numerous stylistic emendations are made to the rapidly composed 1915 version, and Azuela corrects some of the many spelling mistakes found in that version. Later in life Azuela commented on the 1920 edition, saying: 'Los retoques y adiciones que le hice fueron sólo para vigorizar personajes o pasajes, pero no por razones de estilo' (*6*, p.142). This is something of an understatement.

There are two other versions of *Los de abajo*. The first is the adaptation of the novel made by Azuela for the theatre (published in *5*, III, pp.9-80) and first staged in 1929 in Mexico City. Azuela was critical of the production and blamed the producer for its shortcomings, even though it won first prize in a competition and brought the playwright the sum of 4000 pesos which he did not decline (*5*, III, pp.1150-51). The second adaptation of the novel was the film version directed by Chano Urueta and first shown in 1940 in Mexico City. Although Azuela did write at least one film script, he appears to have had nothing to do with the screenplay of *Los de abajo* (*5*, III, pp.1162-65).

It is, of course, the extensively revised novelistic version of *Los de abajo* which is the subject of this Critical Guide.

*   *   *   *   *

Although *Los de abajo* was to set the tone of a spate of novels about the Revolution subsequently produced by Mexican writers, particularly in the 1930s, it had met with critical indifference both when it first appeared in 1915 and when the revised version was published in 1920. It was not until 1924 and 1925, when a debate took place among Mexican intellectuals about whether modern Mexican literature existed and whether a novel had been written which truly depicted their Revolution, that *Los de abajo* (and, to a lesser extent, other works by Azuela) attracted the attention of critics and the reading public. Even then, it was only by chance that a friend of Azuela's children, who happened to have read his novels, published an interview in which a leading Mexican critic praised *Los de abajo*, thus drawing attention to it. The novel was favourably reviewed, figured at the centre of a literary dispute, and was subsequently reprinted in Mexico, appearing also in a Spanish edition (Madrid, 1927), and being translated abroad (*15*, pp.53-62).[5] But by then,

---

[5] After the public recognition of *Los de abajo* in the 1920s, it suited Mexican institutions to promote Azuela as a national figure and representative writer of the Mexican Revolution. His fame rested mainly upon *Los de abajo* although, in reality, he was prolific and wrote on a wide range of subjects

discouraged by the lack of public or critical response to any of the works which he had written about the Revolution, Azuela had abandoned the subject and the literary method he had developed for its portrayal.

---

and in a variety of styles. Despite the public honours he received, he was always wary of being identified with the post-revolutionary establishment in Mexico (*14*).

2. *Reality and Realism*

It was noted at the beginning of Chapter 1 that in *Los de abajo*, as in several of his other novels, Azuela presents the reader with a remarkably accurate fictionalization of many Mexicans' experience during the Revolution. The development and fate of Macías and his column, in a careful interweaving of history and fiction, parallels the course of the Revolution. The first Part of the novel depicts the final stages of Huerta's regime lived out by a small band of predominantly rural fighters; Parts II and III portray the fragmentation after the victory at Zacatecas of the forces opposed to Huerta, and the defeat of the *villistas* as they attempted in vain to resist Obregón's *constitucionalista* advance. In the course of the novel historical events are alluded to. To take just three examples, there is Natera's abortive attack on Zacatecas (124, 127), followed by the arrival of Villa's famous División del Norte which, in June 1914, finished the job bungled by Natera (129-36); the gathering of major and minor revolutionary leaders for the Aguascalientes Convention in October 1914 (171, 174, 176-80); and Villa's defeat at Celaya in April 1915 (184-86).

Within this historical framework, Azuela mirrors major trends in the Revolution. In the early stages of the Revolution, irregular forces led by *caudillos* like Demetrio Macías operated autonomously in their native regions, often being little more than bandits even though they enjoyed the support of the local population; in the novel, Macías's raggle-taggle band is sheltered and fed in Camila's village. As time went on, such groups of irregulars were gradually militarized and incorporated into the mainstream of the *constitucionalista* armed opposition to Huerta, and, once again, this is reflected in the novel where Macías's ex-convicts, criminals on the run, and *rancheros* in dispute with their local *caciques* are originally dubbed 'los hombres de Demetrio Macías' (79), but soon become 'rebeldes' and even 'soldados' (99). In a similar vein, Macías, initially referred to as their 'jefe', is transformed, once they emerge from the hills for the combined attack on Zacatecas, into a colonel (124), and subsequently promoted to the rank of general (139). After the victory of that campaign, Azuela describes some of Macías's veterans and his recent recruits as they set off for Moyahua, sated with food, drink, sex and pillage, in the following ironic terms: 'Demetrio Macías con su *Estado Mayor*: el *coronel* Anastasio Montañés, el *teniente coronel* Pancracio y los *mayores* Luis Cervantes y el güero Margarito' (150; my italics). Thus it is that Demetrio's horn (77) is replaced by bugles (150), and his followers are now referred to as a 'cuerpo de ejército' (163). After Obregón's series of victories in 1915, the *villistas* reverted in the main to guerrilla activity and banditry, often sacking the very villages from which they had drawn their early support. In Part III of *Los de abajo* we see Macías's men preying on the population of their home territory, the *sierra*, which had been devastated by the constant depredations of the opposing armies.

Similarly, as we have seen, after the fall of Huerta, strife broke out between the *constitucionalista* and the *convencionista* factions. The decision to join one side or the other was often arbitrary, each faction being composed of many strange bed-fellows, and the unfolding of the military campaigns was unpredictable and chaotic. As we shall see in Chapter 4, Azuela mirrors this structurally in the apparently formless second Part of the novel with its aimless wandering, killing, looting, and the volatile moods of the revolutionaries, alternating as they do between sadism and mercy, depression and elation.

Yet the historical reliability of Azuela's novel is not confined to the framework of events within which he sets the action of *Los de abajo* nor to the broader trends of the Revolution. The novel is full of telling details which allude, often only in passing, to important aspects of the Revolution that would have been familiar to contemporary readers in Mexico (indeed, he claimed never to have written a single line intended for foreigners and assumes that his public shares his first-hand knowledge of the Revolution). The hatred of Federal Army press-gangs (*la leva*) (83, 89, 118) and the way in which village women had to cope when all the men had been conscripted (84-113); the unreliability of the conscript troops, ever ready to desert (89, 118, 121); the freedom which fighting in the Revolution brought to millions of Mexicans accustomed to an endless round of agricultural labours or to virtual slavery on the *haciendas* (113, 114, 150, 195); the dangers of appearing too well-dressed when the revolutionaries were in town (176); the revolution-aries' scorn for the poor performance of the *federales* on the battle-field (160); the later recruitment of ex-*federal* officers into the *villista* armies (187); the primitive military tactics of the *villistas* which brought them early successes but would eventually lead to their defeat (116, 133); the isolation of the small bands of rebels who learnt about major events of the Revolution in a piecemeal and arbitrary fashion (104, 115, 184); the massacres of prisoners and of virtually defenceless opponents (161); the anti-clericalism which was particularly prevalent in 1914 and 1915 (see below, p.93); and the war-weariness, hunger and disease portrayed at the end of the novel (182, 183-84, 190, 192, 194-95) all mirror historical reality.

Azuela also offers a perceptive insight into many revolution-aries' motives for joining the uprising. In the first chapter of the novel Demetrio Macías abandons his home because he is hounded by the *federales*, and in the second, he places the blame for this persecution squarely on his local *cacique*, Don Mónico: 'En Moyahua está el cacique que me trae corriendo por los cerros' (77). He would later claim to Cervantes that Don Mónico had falsely denounced him to the Federal Army as a dangerous *maderista* because he had stood up to the *cacique* in a dispute and had spat in his face, and that Don Mónico had led a detachment of Federal troops from Zacatecas to arrest him, only to find that he had fled (107). There is no revolutionary zeal here, but rather a local grievance of the sort which motivated many of the participants in the Mexican Revolution; it is scarcely surprising that Macías's first action after the battle of Zacatecas — when the regime which supported *caciques* like Don Mónico has been swept aside — is to return to his native region to settle his score with the *cacique*. This picture is especially true of Azuela's native state of Jalisco where the local population was particularly slow to join the Revolution. There is no indication that Demetrio — who is from Limón, virtually on the border between the states of Jalisco and Zacatecas — had been inclined to do so nor that, even when he is caught up in the mainstream of the Revolution, he believes himself to be taking part in any sort of movement motivated by economic or political factors. The description given by the narrator and by Macías himself of his home suggests that he is a reluctant revolutionary. Macías's men are ignorant about the background to the Revolution (e.g. 86, 160, 180) but, as Azuela makes clear, it is not merely that their ignorance makes them unaware of their involvement in an ideological struggle. The placing in Cervantes's mouth of the claim that Macías is an unconscious representative of some transcendental movement — 'Somos elementos de un gran movimiento social que tiene que concluir por el engrandecimiento de nuestra patria. Somos instrumentos del destino para la reivindicación de los sagrados derechos del pueblo' (109) — and the style in which Cervantes couches it suggest that such an interpretation is nothing but humbug. Luis Cervantes depicts the revolutionaries as having lived a life of suffering and exploitation before the Revolution, but we have learnt to treat with suspicion any statement from this source. Macías, by contrast, maintains that he wanted for nothing, being entirely contented as long as he was left to get on with his life undisturbed (105, 107). He owned land and livestock (165), had prepared his fields for sowing (165), and — although the description of his house indicates what we might consider poverty (73) — he claims that he had money to buy all he needed, never going hungry (105): he is able to provide his men with drink and salt, and even his dog is well fed (78, 79, 74). Before the corrosive influence of the Revolution affects him, his ambition is to return to his land and his family, there to live in peace and what he clearly thinks of as prosperity (107). Far from being a representative of the rural discontent which did, indeed, exist in much of Mexico, or of any supposed class antagonism, Macías, like many of the Jalisco *rancheros* who were swept along by the Revolution, is merely an 'hoja seca arrebatada por el vendaval' (126), an unwilling revolutionary caught up in the wider turmoil for purely personal local reasons. Azuela is also at pains to stress that, despite the fact that the most despicable members of Demetrio's band show resentment of the 'catrines', they are entirely indifferent to any call from their fellow peasants and feel no class or racial solidarity (98); it is not fortuitous that, in a telling scene, Demetrio the full-blood Indian mercilessly butchers a fellow Indian who has spied for the *federales* (123).

Azuela's account of those major historical events to which he chooses to allude, of the broad trends in the development of the Revolution, of the atmosphere of the period, and of the motives and attitudes of the *rancheros* of his part of the country is a faithful one. This does not mean, however, that *Los de abajo* is mere *reportage*. When Azuela maintains, as he frequently does in his letters and memoirs, that his novel is truthful he means that he has done something more than simply getting his facts right.

Some critics have been dismissive of any attempt to place Azuela within a tradition of literary creation, but authors are readers, and it would be surprising if what they read had no influence on what they wrote. The higher generalities of an age — philosophical, scientific, ideological and esthetic — affect a writer's view of the world and how he portrays it. When Azuela asserts that *Los de abajo* is a truthful reflection of the Mexican Revolution he is echoing ideas which have a long tradition; his insistence upon the truth of his novels, and, indeed, the very assumption that novels can provide a true representation of people and events derives from theories which underlay the works of nineteenth-century realist and naturalist writers.

Realism and naturalism are notoriously elastic terms. Nevertheless, Azuela confidently talks of composing realist novels and of having been influenced by realist authors (5, III, p.1130). He claims to have read widely in European realism and naturalism — Balzac, the Goncourts, Zola, Daudet, Flaubert, Maupassant, Galdós and Alas (Clarín) were among his favourite writers — and, in his own statements about his methods, aims and techniques, many of his ideas reflect the theory and practice of nineteenth-century European realists, particularly the French. Broadly speaking, nineteenth-century realism in France was characterized firstly by authors' meticulous research into the subjects they wished to treat, such documentation providing, they felt, a necessary antidote to the romantic imagination which had previously been so important, and enabling them, at least theoretically, to give an accurate account of the contemporary world; and secondly by a close observation of everyday reality, with writers training themselves to capture in words the uniqueness of each object or person. Realist writers, like the naturalists, believed that art was a mimetic representation of external reality and they frequently used their works as vehicles for social or ideological comment. The major distinguishing feature of naturalism, which developed out of realism, was the application to the novel of contemporary scientific theories, in particular those of Taine who believed that human behaviour was merely a product of race (or heredity), environment, and immediate circumstances. As human behaviour was mechanically determined by external forces (determinism is a notable feature of much naturalist literature), the writer could, in theory, eschew any moral judgement of his characters and observe them objectively in the same way that a scientist was assumed to be capable of objectivity in the examination of a specimen (although percipient writers were aware that absolute objectivity was impossible to achieve). In his important essay on the contemporary novel, *Le Roman* (written in 1887), Maupassant stated:

> The novelist [...] who attempts to give us an accurate picture of life must be careful to avoid in his plot any linking of events which would strike us as implausible. His aim is not to tell us a story, to entertain us or arouse compassion, but to oblige us to think, to make us perceive the deeply hidden meaning behind events. Through having thought and observed, he has acquired a personal vision of the world, of things and people, a vision derived from the sum of his observations and his

reflections upon them. It is this personal vision of the world which he tries to convey to us by embodying it in a book. He must reproduce life with scrupulous accuracy if he is to move us in the same way that the spectacle of life has moved him. He will therefore have to write his work so subtly, disguising his art so carefully, and giving the appearance of such simplicity, that it is impossible to perceive and point out the overall design or to discover his intentions.

Not only does Maupassant dismiss the crude notion of novels being mere *reportage*, but he also alludes to characteristics typical of many realist and naturalist works: the creation of an illusion of reality; the preference for the seemingly authentic slice of life rather than implausible plots (often, in turn, leading to a predilection for unremarkable characters and events portrayed in an apparently unstructured narrative, such a focus creating the impression of truth to life because the banal is more typical than accounts of heroes and great deeds); apparent simplicity; and the insight afforded by the novels into the significance of and the causes behind events.

This is necessarily an over-simplified sketch of the theories and practice of the French realists and naturalists. Many of their works display only some of these characteristics as well, of course, as many more, and there is considerable overlap between realist and naturalist practice. However, it is important to note how closely these broad ideas are reflected in Azuela's writings on the novel and in *Los de abajo*.

Azuela said that he always based his writings upon his own experiences or upon those he had heard about from witnesses: 'Aunque mis escritos han sido de mera imaginación, los he basado siempre en hechos de los que he sido testigo o me han contado en forma viva y fidedigna. Me es más fácil reconstruir que inventar' (5, III, p.1102). He followed the realists' injunction that the author should document himself thoroughly and draw upon his own close observation. He tells us, for example, that in preparation for writing his *Pedro Moreno, el insurgente* (published as a newspaper serial in

1933 and 1934), he undertook conscientious research: he read all the relevant historical material, visited the site of Moreno's last stand, and paid close attention to detail, studying, for instance, the flora and fauna of the region and even noting their local names (5, III, pp.1102-03). Azuela appears to have employed similar methods for *Los de abajo*. As it deals, in true realist fashion, with contemporary life, Azuela could not use written historical sources but drew upon his own experiences or the reports of participants to whom he spoke. He had, for example, still been at Lagos when Villa stormed Zacatecas, and he therefore had no opportunity to see for himself the battle which was going to figure at a key moment of the novel. He therefore listened out for first-hand accounts from Medina's men when he joined them at Irapuato, and reworked these reports into the description we are given in Chapter 21 of the first Part. Similarly, Chapters 16 and 17 of Part I of *Los de abajo* appear to have been based upon eye-witness reports of General Leocadio Parra's and Manuel Caloca's attack on *carrancista* troops in the town of San Miguel el Alto. Most of the novel, however, is certainly based upon personal observation. As pointed out in the previous chapter, Azuela claims that one reason for joining Medina's forces was his desire to obtain material for a book he wanted to write about the Revolution:

> Desde que se inició el movimiento con Madero, sentí un gran deseo de convivir con auténticos revolucionarios — no de discursos, sino de rifles — como material humano inestimable para componer un libro, de suerte que esa sola circunstancia me bastaba para sentir placer y satisfacción en mi forzada aventura [...] Satisfice entonces uno de mis mayores anhelos, convivir con los genuinos revolucionarios, los de abajo. (5, III, pp.1080, 1268)

His experiences gave him the opportunity to observe the Revolution and the revolutionaries at close quarters: his memoirs frequently refer to the notebook he carried with him everywhere in which he jotted down the notes that would be worked up into *Los de abajo*.

His experiences during June and July 1915 provided much of the material that would be incorporated into the novel. We have already seen that he made word-sketches during his circuitous journey from Tepatitlán to Aguascalientes, and he even claims, somewhat picturesquely, that when Caloca's band were under attack from *carrancistas* in the Juchipila canyon, he took cover from the gunfire in a cave, notebook in hand, and scribbled down the descriptions which he would later use for the final chapter of the novel (*5*, III, p.1087).

However, Azuela was aware that the realist novel is not composed of unmediated *reportage*. Documentation and observation are necessarily selective because the author's experience is limited (*6*, p.275), and they are reworked by the creative imagination into something which can be true in a deeper sense than merely being factually accurate: a work of fiction presents the reader with Maupassant's 'personal vision' of reality. Although the writer should be self-effacing, concealing his art, this vision moulds his documented and observed material so that, while creating an illusion of reality, the novel does not reproduce the world but, rather, illuminates and interprets it from a particular perspective, be it moral, ideological or whatever (*27*, pp.144-52). As Azuela put it in an essay on Proust, 'el artista [...] por la magia de su fuerza creadora logra que otros vean en el mundo lo que *él sí ha visto*, pero los demás sólo pueden ver cuando se les sabe mostrar' (*5*, III, p.959). In Maupassant's words, he 'makes us perceive the deeply hidden meaning behind events'. This meaning is, as Azuela well knew, subjective (*5*, III, p.1124).

There is a key speech made by Solís in Chapter 18, Part I, of *Los de abajo* in reply to Cervantes's enquiry about what events had led to his disillusion with the Revolution:

> — ¿Hechos?... Insignificancias, naderías: gestos inadvertidos para los más; la vida instantánea de una línea que se contrae, de unos ojos que brillan, de unos labios que se pliegan; el significado fugaz de una frase que se pierde. Pero hechos, gestos y expresiones que, agrupados

en su lógica y natural expresión, constituyen e integran
una mueca pavorosa y grotesca a la vez de una raza...
¡De una raza irredenta! (126)

We shall have occasion to return to this passage. Here, however, it
may be seen as a cameo of the creative process outlined above:
Solís, an intellectual who attempts to make sense of the Revolution
in a way that the common soldiers do not, has keenly observed his
comrades. He arranges these observations to form a fragmentary but
coherent case study, interprets the symptoms, and thus reaches a
diagnosis of the ills of the nation. It is not for nothing that Azuela
was a doctor, and the process described by Solís is similar to
Azuela's own account of the composition of *Los de abajo*: 'Podría
decir que este libro se hizo solo y que mi labor consistió en
coleccionar tipos, gestos, paisajes y sucedidos, si mi imaginación no
me hubiese ayudado a ordenarlos' *(5,* III, p.1078). Azuela claimed
that, although greatly influenced by French realism in his early work,
he had broken with it in his novels and stories about the Revolution
(*5,* III, p.1280; see also *19,* pp.58-59). He comments:

> dejé de ser [...] el observador sereno e imparcial que me
> había propuesto en mis cuatro primeras novelas. Ora
> como testigo, ora como actor en los sucesos que
> sucesivamente me servirían de base para mis escritos,
> tuve que ser y lo fui de hecho, un narrador parcial y
> apasionado. (*5,* III, p.1070)

It is true that *Los de abajo* is an indignant novel into which the
author not only infuses a personal view of the Revolution but also
occasionally intrudes in a somewhat indecorous manner, and in
which certain characters are pilloried with an irony so trenchant as to
approximate to sarcasm. Nevertheless, as we have seen, impartiality
is not, and indeed never could be, a feature of the realist novel. Yet,
although he was passionately convinced that the Revolution had
been betrayed by self-seekers and much of his work is devoted to
unmasking and satirizing these opportunists, Azuela generally

refrains from preaching. Indeed, he felt that one of the major defects of the Mexican novel had been its tendency to sermonize and, for most of the novel, he appears to present us with an honest and succinct account, and then leave us to draw our own conclusions about it, although, in reality, he is directing what those conclusions will be. However clear the condemnation of the waste, anarchy and corruption of the Revolution implied in his novels, and however much they depict that Revolution in a manner which rejected slavish imitation of European realism, they still owe much to the French authors Azuela admired, as a study of *Los de abajo* reveals.

Firstly, as has been noted, it is factually accurate and well documented. Secondly, much of it is based upon personal observation. Thirdly, the plot is deliberately unremarkable: the capture of Zacatecas — a pivotal event in the Revolution — is relegated to a fragmentary report put in the mouth of a disillusioned witness, and the final stages of the battle take place in the gap between Parts I and II of the novel. In the last chapter of Part II Azuela describes the anonymous mass of participants travelling to Aguascalientes, but offers no glimpse of the Convention itself. The crucial battles of Celaya are merely recounted to Macías's incredulous band by four deserters from Villa's army. By alluding only in passing to events which would later be given prominence in the official mythification of the Revolution, Azuela allows the reader to learn of them just as the majority of simple fighters must have done. Indeed, not only are heroic engagements generally omitted but very little actually happens in the novel. The characters merely wander from one skirmish or bar to another, and we hear of the death of three of them only from a laconic reference in a reply to a letter which, we are left to assume, contained fuller details (181). Much of the action of the novel takes place in anonymous villages or on unparticularized roads, again depicting the typical rather than the exceptional. The plot is not fanciful, there being no contrived coincidences or peripities, and no major historical figure makes an appearance (with the exception of Pánfilo Natera who utters no more than seven sentences in the entire novel). But *Los de abajo* illustrates how novelists can record what often eludes the historian: the effect of events upon the lives and attitudes of insignificant individuals, and the ambiguities, complexities and arbitrariness of events as they are experienced at the time by the common man, rather than as they are reconstructed later by the historian (*10*, p.15). This is an important feature of the nineteenth-century realist novel:

> It was a realistic novelist (Stendhal) who first consciously presented a de-centred account of a major historical event — the Battle of Waterloo. He showed such an event being experienced by its participants not as a coherent totality but as an often confusing and frequently unintelligible succession of smaller events. And this in turn inspired Tolstoy to de-centre history in perhaps the greatest nineteenth-century realist novel. History, Tolstoy demonstrated, does not revolve around individuals, not even supposedly great individuals; nor does it turn on individual decisions; nor, even, does it consist of epochal occurrences with clearly defined outlines. The 'great man', 'decisive event', vision of history is an artefact of hindsight.[6]

Fourthly, the ordering of events in *Los de abajo* appears merely episodic. I shall suggest in Chapter 4 that Azuela structures the novel with some care but, even if I am justified in my assertions there, the elusiveness of narrative patterns illustrates the author's 'disguising his art so carefully, and giving the appearance of such simplicity, that it is [almost] impossible to perceive and point out the overall design'. We are certainly not left with an impression of a heavy authorial hand intervening to falsify reality for the sake of artistic symmetry.

Fifthly, Azuela writes in a simple, straightforward fashion. The style of the narrative sections does not call attention to itself in a way which would suggest that the author wishes us to admire the novel for any stylistic *tours de force* it might contain. However, such

---

[6]Raymond Tallis, *In Defence of Realism* (London: Edward Arnold, 1988), p.71.

simplicity is not artless; it is the result of a careful cultivation of a terse style (see below, pp.96-97).

Sixthly, a moral vision filters through the soberly narrated action. Although Azuela sympathizes with the poor and oppressed, his vision of the Revolution is a pessimistic one which not only depicts the revolutionaries' resignation in the face of horror and destruction, but also conveys a deterministic view of events which are likened to the natural cataclysms that men are powerless to prevent. He does not, therefore, aspire to being a dispassionate reporter 'sino [un] novelista que procuró captar más que hombres, cosas y sucesos, la honda significación de los mismos' (5, III, p.1078). It is this interpretation of the Revolution which has been attacked by many later critics who, although they did not witness the turmoil at first hand as Azuela did, nevertheless believe the Revolution to have been more coherent or more positive than he did (e.g. *12*, pp.221, 223; *21*, pp.39, 43).

There is, in addition, one characteristic which Azuela shares with the French naturalists rather than with the realist writers: a concentration upon physiological functions, human degradation, and squalor. *Los de abajo* focuses on such features: we have, for example, menstruation (96), incest (96), delousing (169), the acrid stench of sweat (176), excreta and rotting garbage (156), the entrails of a freshly killed bird being spread on Macías's chest (97), a septic wound (99), deformity (163), the symptoms of venereal disease (129, 142, 151), the sound of a lethal knife entering its victim's rib cage (123), a graphic cameo of ragged women stripping warm and bloody corpses after a battle (133), and depictions of drunkenness (there is much drinking in the novel), lust, gluttony and sadism.

In later chapters of this study I shall describe some of the ways in which Azuela's realism in *Los de abajo* is innovatory. Here we have seen that it is nevertheless firmly rooted in the works of his nineteenth-century predecessors. Perhaps the best example of his debt to those predecessors is his treatment of character and his examination of the way in which individuals are influenced by social and historical circumstances.

3. Characterization and Character

Azuela maintains that many of the characters of *Los de abajo* were modelled upon real people he observed during the Revolution: Anastasio Montañés is apparently based upon a close aide and advisor to Medina, Pancracio upon the most odious soldier the author encountered among his comrades, La Pintada upon the mistress of a revolutionary colonel he met near Juchipila, Venancio upon a pretentious quack, and Valderrama upon Azuela's friend José Becerra. However, as with the creative process we have already examined, in which the author takes elements from observed reality as the raw material from which he fashions something completely different, so Azuela's models bear only an indirect relationship to the novel's characters. Although he shares certain characteristics with both Julián Medina and Manuel Caloca, Demetrio Macías is primarily a product of Azuela's imagination; Luis Cervantes is based only in part on what was, in any case, an unflattering portrait of Medina's personal secretary painted by his enemies; and El güero Margarito is an amalgam of at least three unsavoury comrades. Other characters, like Camila, are apparently entirely fictitious (5, III, pp.1080-86).

As we should expect in any novel, some of Azuela's creatures are types. Nevertheless, it is unjust to dismiss most of them as nothing more than a combination of characteristics which Azuela thought typical of peasants, or to maintain, as some critics have done, that as a bourgeois writer Azuela was incapable of any insight into his peasant characters and accordingly was unable to portray them convincingly. It is similarly unfair to claim that he despised his creations. Azuela went as far as to state: 'Si yo me hubiera encontrado entre los revolucionarios un tipo de la talla de Demetrio Macías, lo habría seguido hasta la muerte' (5, III, p.1082). Although his comments on his own writings are not always reliable — he does on occasion adopt a somewhat condescending or even sarcastic attitude to his characters, as when he describes Camila as 'de rostro muy vulgar' (84), talks of Demetrio's and Venancio's 'rudos cerebros' (182) or depicts the revolutionaries as uncouth clowns (145-46) — it would be imprudent to dismiss out of hand his claim that he was sympathetic towards, and even admired, some of the peasants he portrayed.

His characters are presented in a variety of manners. Azuela maintains that the labelling technique of characterization, in which a physical and psychological portrait is given as soon as a character is introduced into the novel, is amateurish. More significantly, he rejects this method because it does not reflect the way we come to know people in real life. He opted instead for what he claimed was a more realistic approach to characterization in which a character is gradually revealed to the reader during the course of the novel (5, III, pp.1015-16). Broadly speaking, the characters of *Los de abajo* are depicted in a behaviouristic manner, that is to say we have few insights into their thoughts, but learn about them from what they do and say, and about the social circumstances which influence them and their actions. We are generally shown them rather than being told about them, and this method both dramatizes the characters and preserves the illusion of authorial detachment based upon direct observation. It does not, however, preclude the use of physical descriptions which have psychological implications. As Maupassant again put it in his essay *Le Roman*, 'realist writers [...] are careful to avoid complex psychological explanations [...] and limit themselves to making characters and events pass before our eyes [...]. Instead of a long explanation of a character's state of mind, they find an action or gesture which is the automatic response of somebody who finds himself in that state of mind and that particular situation'. The examination of faces is a traditional means of characterization in literature and is, of course, one of the ways we assess other people in everyday life. Nevertheless, among some nineteenth-century thinkers, and consequently among realist and naturalist writers influenced by their ideas, the study of physical characteristics as a key to the inner person — the most extreme form of which was phrenology (the investigation of an individual's psychology through the study of the shape and contours of his skull) — took on the status of a science. Balzac, praised by Azuela as the 'novelista más grande de todos los tiempos' (5, III, p.812), is particularly associated with this method of characterization. When this is coupled with Taine's ideas about the factors determining human psychology, and with widely accepted positivist medical theories — all likely to appeal to a scientifically-trained writer like Azuela — we have something more than a merely traditional method of characterization. In his first novel, *María Luisa* (1907), Azuela offers a pathological examination of a hereditary weakness — the errant gene in this case resulting in a tendency to alcoholism — and, in true positivist fashion, he suggests the physiological origins of psychic states. Although these ideas were less prominent by the time he wrote *Los de abajo*, we do occasionally glimpse them: El Manteca's impulsive and violent behaviour, it is hinted, may be due to epilepsy (103), Margarito's perversion is clinically observed, Azuela perceptively associating sadism with sexual excitement and hinting at the mental imbalance which will eventually lead to his suicide (162), and, as we shall see in Chapter 4, much of the novel dramatizes what Solís claims are inherent, or racial, psychic flaws in all Mexicans (126, 135). This attention to racial defects, together with Azuela's comment about a later novel that, 'Dar un trasunto del *medio* y del *momento* que he estado viviendo ha sido uno de los propósitos fundamentales de la mayor parte de mis novelas' (5, III, p.1098; my italics), cannot fail to bring to mind Taine's theories.

Let us examine how realist and, in particular, naturalist methods of characterization, rooted as they are in nineteenth-century ideas, are employed in *Los de abajo*.

After Luis Cervantes has been captured by Macías's men who believe him to be a *federal* spy, he recalls with horror the faces of Pancracio and El Manteca (it is significant that Azuela uses the word 'fisionomías' here, for the nineteenth-century student of the human face referred to himself as a physiognomist):

Uno, Pancracio, agüerado, pecoso, su cara lampiña, su
barba saltona, la frente roma y oblicua, untadas las orejas
al cráneo y todo de un aspecto bestial. Y el otro, el
Manteca, una piltrafa humana: ojos escondidos, mirada
torva, cabellos muy lacios cayéndole a la nuca, sobre la
frente y las orejas; sus labios de escrofuloso entreabier-
tos eternamente. (90)

Similar descriptions are given of what Azuela was later to dub 'el
pitecántropo, ese tipo que abundó tanto en los días de la revolución'
(5, III, p.1085), Pancracio having a 'duro perfil de prognato' (82 —
note again the scientific vocabulary). La Pintada has 'una frente
pequeña' (138) — a sure sign of baseness to a physiognomist.
Although Azuela may appear here merely to be reporting observable
features, the descriptions he provides prejudice the reader against
these characters. In a similar fashion, we are automatically well
disposed towards Solís when he is introduced as '[un] joven, de
semblante abierto y cordial' (124).

Azuela may have wanted to avoid a simple labelling technique
of characterization, but he was faced by a dilemma when depicting
Macías and his men. While we are offered privileged insights into
Cervantes's meditations, we are seldom permitted a glimpse of the
peasants' thoughts (one exception is the occasional simple insight
into Macías's mind, but even here his thoughts are more pictorial
than analytical; e.g. 76-77, 165). Some critics have deduced from
this that Azuela is dismissive of or fails to understand his revolutionaries (32, p.126). Others have maintained that he is reluctant to enter
the peasants' minds because he is aware that he does not know how
such people really think; his reluctance would, then, be a sign both
of his alienation from the peasantry and of his integrity (21, p.44).
But another explanation is that he had observed that the peasant
revolutionaries were impulsive men of action not given to discursive
analysis of their situation, and, as a realist writer whose aim was to
avoid distorting reality, he chose to portray them as such. After all,
they quickly become impatient when reasoning threatens to postpone
action, and they criticize Cervantes for being nothing but talk (93,

116, 156). Indeed, the insights we are given into Cervantes's thoughts lead us to share their view of him, and we remember that one of Azuela's main criticisms of the course of Mexican history after the death of Madero was that silver-tongued intellectuals had hijacked the Revolution at the expense of the common people. The insights we are allowed into Cervantes's mind reveal the gap between what he professes to believe and what he really thinks; the peasants, by comparison, are straightforward and spontaneous, not devious and calculating (*9*, pp.50-51). Azuela therefore characterizes them by appearance, action, and speech. It is in this way that the more rounded of the peasants are individualized, but the reader has to be alert to appreciate the nuances of Azuela's characterization, and should bring to the novel the same sort of willingness to read imaginatively between the lines that is required when we read the script of a play.

Demetrio Macías is decisive, even impulsive, when involved in military action, for which he has a sure instinct (e.g. 109, 120), but he is hesitant and bewildered when faced with more abstract problems. Azuela embodies the latter characteristic not in the form of a silent soliloquy nor, in the main, in authorial comment, but in a conventional enough physical action: when Demetrio is trying to grasp a problem or make up his mind, he scratches his head (e.g. 87, 93, 108, 120, 180). More subtly, Azuela uses changing facial expression to denote in his characters a range of emotions — usually despicable — which are not spelled out for us; we are left to grasp the significance of the fleeting expressions and to draw our own conclusions about characters from them, much as Solís had done when he said that, by observing the momentary gleam in his comrades' eyes or an ephemeral smile upon their lips, he had deduced that Mexicans were a doomed race (126 and above, pp.37-38) Solís's remarks are always instructive, and his statement leads the reader to pay particular attention to facial expressions, especially eyes and smiles. For example, eyes can convey sexual desire (138, 139, 145, 148), rapacity (108, 142, 157, 168, 177), fear, apprehension or bewilderment (121, 123, 145, 147, 148, 152, 162, 180, 193), sadism and blood-lust (82, 162, 168), indecision (172-73), madness

(189), perspicacity (142, 184), hunger and hatred (193), evil (144), and amoral indifference (82, 123). It is no coincidence that the only indication given at the end of the novel that Macías is dead is the statement 'Demetrio Macías, *con los ojos fijos para siempre*, sigue apuntando con el cañón de su fusil' (197; my italics). In a similar manner, smiles and laughter — there is a good deal of the latter in this grim novel — suggest scorn (75, 135), the pleasurable anticipation of blood-letting (121, 151, 175), delight in the power which superior force confers over one's victims (152, 153), the fearful desire to ingratiate oneself with the powerful (169, 174), the savour of cruelty (170, 171), and revenge (183). Azuela also uses other facial expressions to convey mood or emotion: 'a Demetrio se le contrajo la frente como si algo muy negro hubiera pasado por sus ojos' (184-85), 'El rostro de la Pintada se granitificó' (172), 'Instantáneamente se demudó el rostro de la Pintada' (170). When Demetrio returns home at the end of the novel, he is tongue-tied and does not respond to his wife's question about abandoning the fighting, yet the description of his face is eloquent: 'La faz de Demetrio se ensombreció' (194). Azuela thus uses physical description to solve the problem of portraying in words people who do not express their feelings verbally (cf. 5, II, p.1078).

Another method of conveying character without resorting to direct authorial intervention to inform the reader about characters' emotions or temperament is again borrowed from the physiog-nomists. As we saw earlier, some nineteenth-century thinkers believed that human actions and emotions were, like those of animals, merely the product of instincts and external forces, and that human beings could consequently be examined objectively as if they were scientific specimens. The use of animal comparisons in literature was increasingly based on the assumption of man's close biological kinship with animals. The characters of *Los de abajo* are frequently depicted through such comparisons, the most obvious implication being that the revolutionaries have been dehumanized, and are as bestial as — or occasionally even more bestial than — the animals with which they live in close proximity. But this method also suggests that Azuela thinks of his peasant characters as more

instinctive than reflexive, and it is notable that he does not compare
Luis Cervantes, Solís or Valderrama to animals. Given the rural
background of most of the characters in the novel, it is perhaps only
natural that they should on occasion describe others in this way: thus
La Pintada likens Demetrio to a 'puerco gordo' (143) and they
describe the Federal troops as 'liebres o guajolotes' (160). However,
the narrator himself frequently employs animal comparisons, particularly when describing the characters' less attractive qualities. For
example, when Demetrio and La Pintada meet 'se miraron cara a cara
como dos perros desconocidos que se olfatean con desconfianza'
(139), El Manteca has 'ojos de culebra' (103), Montañés possesses 'la
amoralidad del chacal' (123), the *soldaderas* are like 'perros
callejeros' (138), the band are 'perros hambrientos' (153), La Pintada
'se volvió un alacrán' (166), a roaringly drunken Demetrio is
compared to a 'toro a media plaza' (148), and the whole band are
likened to colts and monkeys (120, 150; see also 77, 84, 133, 179,
184). Somewhat more subtly, Azuela insinuates into his description
of the peasants vocabulary associated with animals — as they squat
down they are 'atejonados' ('acochinados' in the first version of the
novel), lying in the sun they are 'alagartados', the women have
'cuadriles' rather than 'caderas' (*4*, p.264) — and, through use of the
same technique, he reveals his indignation at the revolutionaries'
behaviour, as they defile all that is beautiful, cultured, and civilized:
'Pancracio [...] dio un *aullido*' (110), 'los soldados *bramaron* de
alegría' (145), '¡Pero tú qué!... ¿Tú qué?... *ululaba* Demetrio irritado'
(148), 'La Pintada seguía *berreando*' (148), or *'ruge* [Demetrio]
como una fiera' (196). Considerably more deft is the way Azuela
suggests a comparison in the minds of his characters between the
young blonde girl to whom Cervantes refers as his *novia*, and La
Pintada's handsome black mare. They are described in similar terms
in the same chapter — 'una muchacha de rara belleza' (144) and 'una
bellísima yegua' (146) — as they are both reluctantly brought into
the riotous banquet held in Macías's honour after the victory at
Zacatecas. This last comparison suggests that, despite Cervantes's
protestations to the contrary, both are considered mere booty to be
exhibited in order to excite the envy of the revolutionaries, and to be

used (indeed, mounted) by their new owners or by whoever can steal them. By comparing an innocent virgin with a mare stolen by a syphilitic camp-follower, Azuela bitterly denounces the band's lack of respect for other human beings and, at the same time, draws a parallel between two characters who are, at first sight, very different: La Pintada and Cervantes.

Various methods are employed to acquaint the reader with the characters. The presentation of Pancracio, for instance, is an example of the realist technique of characterization recommended by Azuela in which a person is gradually revealed as we see him talking and acting in different situations. Pancracio first appears in Chapter 3 of the first Part as a simple member of Macías's band; he is not differentiated from the others at this stage except by a brief description of his face: 'su cara lampiña, inmutable como piedra' (81) both suggests that he is of Indian descent and gives a hint of the mercilessness we shall later discover in him. He is, however, an unknown quantity; we are given no indication of his background or of his motives for joining the band. His principal characteristics, brutish ignorance and sadism, are suggested in passing in Chapter 4 (82) and in Chapter 5 (86), but it is not until the following chapter that the reader is offered a reasonably full description of his appearance which proves to be a physical manifestation of his almost sub-human character (90). Little by little a more detailed picture emerges: he is quick to anger, violent, and foul-mouthed (103), he is the first to take advantage of the defenceless, indulge his blood-lust or engage in wanton destruction (e.g. 117, 123, 141), and he gradually takes on the role of the band's lackey (109, 129, 141, 144, 147, 160, 168). The reader is provided with repeated evidence of his sadism until, in the fifth chapter of Part II, Azuela intervenes in a somewhat heavy-handed manner to portray him, albeit through others' eyes, as the archetypal figure of merciless cruelty: 'Las señoras [...] vuelven sus ojos suplicatorios hacia el más cercano de los soldados; pero luego los aprietan con horror: ¡han visto al sayón que está crucificando a Nuestro Señor Jesucristo en la vía crucis de la parroquia!... ¡Han visto a Pancracio!' (152).

Not all the characters are revealed as gradually as this. Although Azuela claimed to disapprove of what I have termed the labelling technique of characterization, such a method is almost unavoidable when an author wishes to give rapidly a modicum of individuality to a minor character whose appearances in a novel are extremely limited. Venancio, for example, is introduced in the following way:

> Venancio era barbero; en su pueblo sacaba muelas y ponía cáusticos y sanguijuelas. Gozaba de cierto ascendiente porque había leído *El judío errante* y *El sol de mayo*. Le llamaban *el dotor*, y él, muy pagado de su sabiduría, era hombre de pocas palabras. (83)

This description summarizes his distinguishing characteristics — arrogance, social ambition, and a false reputation for learning based upon his literacy and quackery. He is the butt of Azuela's irony and of the other characters' laughter for the rest of the novel. Little more is discovered about Venancio except that he affects a gravity commensurate with his view of his status, and that his motive for joining Macías was, according to La Codorniz, a need to escape from his village after he had poisoned his *novia* by administering an aphrodisiac to her (98).

This allegation of Venancio's motives illustrates a further technique: we learn about Azuela's characters from the way they react to and speak of each other, for comments made by one character about another often tell us more about the speaker than about his subject. When Margarito refers to La Pintada as 'esta chinche' (173), he provides a telling comment about her, for she, like Cervantes, is indeed a parasite who feeds upon Macías's band. However, Margarito's statement tells us much more about him: we realize that he is astute and disloyal enough to distance himself from his old companion as soon as he is aware that she has been rejected by Demetrio and his men. This may be straightforward enough, but it can become a good deal more subtle, as is revealed by the form of address which the characters use with each other.[7] With the exception of Demetrio's wife and La Pintada (once the latter and Demetrio have become sexual partners), all the other characters, including Cervantes, use 'usted' with Macías — a clear indication of the respect he inspires in his men, who use the familiar form among themselves. From his first appearance in the novel, Cervantes, on the other hand, employs a condescending familiarity with all the other members of the band except Venancio who, he is quick to realize, is a powerful influence over Macías and with whom he therefore curries favour by flattery and by addressing him with hypocritical respect. In his turn Cervantes, as well as the other figure from the city, Margarito, is referred to as 'usted' by Demetrio. Even La Pintada uses 'usted' to Cervantes, openly acknowledging her awareness of the class gulf between him and the rest of the band (149). Camila initially addresses him formally, slips into a familiarity to which Azuela draws the reader's attention (94), but returns to the 'usted' form once she has been tricked by Cervantes into becoming Demetrio's woman. Demetrio himself employs the familiar form with most of his band, reflecting his role as their protector and leader (a position also symbolized by his providing them with salt in Chapter 2 of Part I). One of the most telling choices of form of address is the 'usted' used between the old *compadres* Demetrio and Anastasio Montañés. It indicates a rural formality which casts a favourable light upon both characters, possibly harking back to a pre-Revolutionary world of honest relationships founded on mutual respect between equals, in contrast to the new world of the Revolution where acquaintance is ephemeral and based upon self-interest. The same is true of Camila and Demetrio who are both from the *sierra* and treat each other with a respectful formality even after they have become lovers (160, 163, 166, 171). Forms of address are therefore significant, for they are a tacit statement of one character's view of another, and tell the reader something about both.

Formality or informality of address implies comparison and contrast between relationships. Such comparison and contrast is an

---

[7]The plural of both familiar and formal forms of address is 'ustedes' in Mexican Spanish.

important aspect of characterization both within a single developing
character and between two or more characters. This is perhaps best
illustrated by a closer examination of two major figures in the novel,
Demetrio Macías and Luis Cervantes.

Demetrio Macías

It is not uncommon for characters, on their first appearance in a
novel, to be presented as recognizable types. Indeed, this may well
be how the author himself first conceives of them. Subsequently, a
character may be individualized, the reader's initial impression either
modified or radically changed, and the character gain a certain
autonomy — Azuela disapproved, at least in theory, of tailoring
characters to fit a thesis (5, III, pp.1042-43, 1147-48). At first
Demetrio Macías is little more than an outline — 'una silueta blanca'
(75) — and is a typical *ranchero* from the *sierras* of Jalisco and
Zacatecas. He demonstrates characteristics which Azuela associated
with this type: 'el tipo genuino del ranchero de Jalisco, valiente,
ingenuo, generoso y fanfarrón' (5, III, p.1079). The first chapter of
the novel, which is a model of concise exposition, prepares the
reader for much that is to come: Demetrio is an Indian (he will later,
114, be described as a full-blood), and he has the Indian's apparent
impassivity and inscrutability, but he is far from being one of the
picturesquely colourful Indians who appear as minor characters in
many Mexican novels written before those of Azuela. Indeed, the
very choice of an Indian as the protagonist of his novel is a measure
of Azuela's innovatory realism. Demetrio is measured in speech and
action, merciful when the garrulous *federal* lieutenant pleads for his
life by invoking his family, fearless, fatalistic, decisive, astute, and
gentle but firm. We learn that he has served a gaol sentence, and that
he enjoys a reputation for bravery and banditry; but he now has a
wife and child, and works his own land in the *sierra*. His origins as a
serrano will remain an intrinsic part of his character throughout the
novel: when he leaves his homeland and descends to the plain, he is
out of his element, uneasy and vulnerable (164). Camila, who is
from his native region and who shares his feelings, is the woman to

whom he is attracted; she, like his wife, fits his ideal of the gentle and submissive partner (165). By contrast, he is out of his depth in the city, with city-dwellers, and with the wild Northern Mexicans who join his band. La Pintada is the epitome of the interloper from the North: she bewilders and, on more than one occasion, unmans him by her brazenness (138-39, 148, 172-73); and she successfully defies him in front of his *serrano* comrades who have always shown him respect (172-73). His descent to the lowlands and his contact with people from outside the *sierras* thus parallel to some extent his decline as his links with his roots are severed by the Revolution.

The early chapters reinforce the positive picture of Demetrio given at the beginning of the novel: he is a loving father and husband; he is respected by the small band of irregulars who gather round him; he is expert in handling them; and he is a skilled marksman and tactician in guerrilla operations. As the novel progresses, however, he develops beyond the stereotype or representative figure. It would be an exaggeration to claim that in Demetrio Macías Azuela provides a profound psychological study; the novel is too short and too concerned with the dynamic narration of events for this. Nevertheless, Demetrio is individualized: we are shown negative as well as positive aspects of his personality, and he emerges as something of an unpredictable and enigmatic figure. He is evidence for Azuela's stated belief that real people — and hence the sort of characters he wished to portray in his realist fiction — are a mixture of vices and virtues: 'en mis correrías de revolucionario acabé de confirmar mi idea de que el hombre exclusivamente bueno o exclusivamente malo sólo existe en las novelas' (5, III, p.1060). Demetrio is incapable of grasping abstract concepts, yet he can be astute about his fellows. He skilfully wins the support of his original comrades and when, for example, Luis Cervantes is introduced, full of bluster and indignant self-importance, Demetrio immediately cuts him down to size and then reduces him to silence (87). When the same man later accuses his comrades of tarnishing the Revolution by unseemly pillaging, Demetrio again cuts him short with a withering stare, making it clear that, coming from a man who has just hidden two stolen diamonds in his pocket, such criticism is humbug (142). Eventually, he gets the full measure of Cervantes and is even able to take advantage of the latter's greed for booty to induce him to fetch Camila (157). Yet he can also be ingenuous: when he arranges a mock confession to test Cervantes, it does not occur to him that Cervantes might see through the charade or that he might lie to the confessor, thus profaning a sacrament (92-93), yet Demetrio sees nothing wrong with sacrilegiously faking a sacrament himself (*32*, p.291). Indeed, his religiosity is mere superstition and is concerned with the outward observance of ritual (105, 120). He knows nothing of political issues: he unashamedly asks Natera to tell him which side of the conflict to join after the Aguascalientes Convention (180), he fails to understand humorous allusive comments (139), and is inept at speaking in public (112). Nevertheless, many of his instincts are honourable, at least in the early part of the book: he wants to treat the villagers of the *sierra* decently by his own lights and to maintain a good reputation among them (110, 155), he can show respect to the downtrodden (164-65), has no desire to profit materially from the turmoil (155), and, as a man with a keen sense of loyalty, he will not abandon the Revolution as Cervantes does when he has amassed a sufficient fortune (156). Azuela is careful to show Demetrio taking no active part in looting and destruction (128) and to portray him as merciful and just in his revenge on Don Mónico: he burns the *cacique*'s house just as the *cacique* had been responsible for burning his, but he does not want it plundered nor blood shed (153-54). Demetrio may be ignorant and inarticulate, but those very characteristics make him appear sincere when contrasted with the dishonourable use to which Cervantes puts his intelligence and gift of the gab, for Azuela is profoundly suspicious of the glib eloquence of city slickers.

Demetrio's love of fighting is neither wholly admirable nor entirely reprehensible. He is one of the heroes of the battle of Zacatecas: an embodiment of the primitive military *élan* which typified the *villistas* as he leads a cavalry charge against the *federales*, lassoing their machine-guns from horseback (a telling image of the old world in conflict with the new, and a tactic which will have fatal consequences when his primitive band is eventually cut down by modern machine-guns in the Juchipila canyon (196), just as were Villa's forces at Celaya). On other occasions, he shows more than a hint of relish at the thought of killing (121) and disgust with an enemy too weak to put up a good fight (160, 161). Nor is he averse to drinking himself senseless. One of the most negative pictures we see of him is when, overcome by alcohol and lust, he attempts to rape a young girl: 'Demetrio, tambaleándose de borracho [...] con los ojos encendidos como una brasa y hebras cristalinas en los burdos labios, buscaba con avidez a la muchacha' (148).

The worst aspects of his character tend, however, to be seen in Part II of the novel as he comes into contact with the world outside his native *sierras*, Azuela suggesting that it is his experience during the Revolution and the people he meets, as much as any inherent flaws in his character, that are to blame for the atrocities he permits. He is easily led by the worst of his comrades: originally by Venancio, then by Cervantes who urges him to join the mainstream of the Revolution, and, for much of Part II, by Margarito and La Pintada. Part II begins with a short statement: 'Al champaña que ebulle en burbujas donde se descompone la luz de los candiles, Demetrio Macías prefiere el límpido tequila de Jalisco' (137). The juxtaposition of the two drinks is not gratuitous; it contrasts the candour and strength of the indigenous *rancheros* of Jalisco with the superficial cities where frothily insubstantial imported luxuries dazzle and corrupt. One might almost say that it contrasts the old Macías with the one who will develop in the Part which this statement introduces. It is an indication of the change wrought in Demetrio that, despite his own preferences, he orders champagne when he is elated by the flattery of self-seekers and the undisguised sexual provocation of La Pintada (139). He becomes untrue to himself and, in the end, will turn a blind eye to his followers' excesses and even to their insubordination (170), something to which, early in Part II, he had reacted decisively (154). Eventually he is deceived and deserted by his own troops (187, 196). Even his image of himself is influenced by outsiders. It was noted earlier that Azuela considered the typical *ranchero* of Jalisco to be a braggart, and Anastasio Montañés certainly possesses this trait, but it seems at

first that such boastfulness is not part of Demetrio's nature.
However, Solís's flattering comments about his heroic feats go to
Demetrio's head (126). A man of few words at the beginning of the
novel, he is puffed up with pride when unknown revolutionaries
praise him (139), he learns to vaunt his feats of arms (144), and at
the end of the novel he even regales his old *compadre* with an exaggerated account of his first engagement with the *federales*,
apparently oblivious of the fact that, as Anastasio had also taken part
in it, he therefore knows what had actually happened (195). Indeed,
the desire to maintain the almost legendary reputation he has gained
by the end of Part I possibly influences his subsequent actions,
accounting in part for his reckless bravery at Zacatecas and his
determination at the end of the novel to carry on fighting even when
the outcome is inevitable (26, 158-66). If this is the case, Azuela is
subtly making the barbed comment that the intellectual's (Solís's)
distortion of the truth is indirectly to blame for Macías's death.
However, Demetrio is susceptible not only to negative influences.
When he is alone with Camila in Chapter 10 of Part II, her effect on
him is striking: he becomes considerate and gentle to her and to
others, and she is later able to improve, even if only momentarily,
his followers' treatment of the weak (169). It is, of course, significant
that this force for good comes from the *sierras* of his home region.

Demetrio is not only easily led by others; his experiences in
the Revolution also teach him a certain indifference and hardness,
illustrated by his changing feelings for his family. In the first chapter
of the novel his parting from his wife and child are movingly
portrayed. In Part II the recollection of this parting moves him to
show mercy to Don Mónico's family (153). But, with time, the
memories of his family are dimmed by separation and his temporary
attachment to other women. Eventually he can no longer even
remember his child's face (165). When he meets his wife again at the
end of the novel, family bonds have been damaged beyond repair: he
looks at his wife almost as if she were a stranger, and the child is
terrified by his father's attempts to embrace him. Demetrio is not
incapable of emotion, but his tears are now provoked by a
sentimental song (189) or by the death of a comrade (196), rather

than by his family. Through Demetrio's reaction to his wife Azuela implicitly comments that the Revolution led to social disintegration and destroyed affective relationships, numbing or deforming men's sensibilities. Similarly, in Demetrio it produces idleness and the desire merely to satisfy physiological needs (143, 155, 156, 169). In Part III, however, Demetrio tends to be seen once more in a positive light, the author thus ensuring that the reader is left with the impression of a fundamentally good man who has been corrupted by the Revolution: the decent individual is unable to resist the pernicious influence of events and of those who surround him.

Demetrio, then, is not an unparticularized type, and he develops, albeit simply, during the course of the novel, his character being established in a variety of ways; one of the most important, as we shall see, is by comparison and contrast with other characters, particularly Cervantes.

Luis Cervantes

Like most of the intellectuals in Azuela's novels concerned with the Revolution, Cervantes is an opportunist who is determined to make his fortune by exploiting the power which superior knowledge confers. In his comments on *Los de abajo* Azuela himself refers to Cervantes as a 'seudorrevolucionario y logrero' (5, III, p.1081), and 'uno de los especímenes más repugnantes de la fauna revolucionaria: el logrero de la revolución que sólo busca su medro personal' (4, p.170), a representative of a new class members of which profited from the Revolution to enrich themselves and gain political influence and who figure prominently in almost all of Azuela's work. He has no redeeming features: he is arrogant (85, 86, 171), greedy (142, 154-55, 157, 168), cowardly (88, 116, 131-32), a flatterer (108, 124), a hypocrite (142), a turncoat (88-90, 125), an intellectual who sold out to the Porfirian establishment and used his position as a journalist slavishly to support it (94, 125), and a thief who cheats his comrades (155). He is also an empty talker (116, 124, 156) and a liar. He claims, for instance, to have been conscripted into the Federal Army as a punishment for his support of the Revolution, but

we soon learn that, in fact, he had volunteered after having written
newspaper articles condemning Huerta's opponents (87, 88); he lies
to Demetrio (110) and Venancio (100, 181), deceives the innocent
Camila (158), and even tries to pull the wool over Solís's eyes (125).
The words 'mentira' and 'mentiroso' are frequently associated with
him (109, 111, 124, 158, 168, etc.), and Camila's ingenuous question
to him, added in the 1920 version, '¿Oye, curro, y tú has de saber
contar cuentos?' (95) is charged with irony. Cervantes is a man who
is so wrapped up in himself and his ambitions that, initially at least,
he is incapable of putting himself imaginatively in the position of
others. It is for this reason that he neither realizes that Camila is
trying to endear herself to him and ingenuously to arouse his jealous
indignation (101-02, 110-12), nor attempts, at least at first, to adapt
his intellectual's language and vacuous rhetoric to his uneducated
listeners who cannot understand what he is saying; he even uses
Latin tags when addressing them (87, 104, 146). Similarly, he is
incapable of believing that others are not motivated by the same
materialistic ends as himself: he accuses Camila of stupidity when
she proves reluctant to give herself to Demetrio despite promises of
wealth (111), and he is almost impervious to Demetrio's sincere
claim that it is not wealth that he is fighting for (155-56).

Cervantes is a necessary figure in the novel, for Azuela
requires somebody to make general comments about the Revolution,
even if his ironic treatment of Cervantes's statements shows them to
be hollow (at the end of Part I Solís is introduced to make more
reliable comments as well as to act as an interlocutor and foil for
Cervantes, and in Part III Valderrama is brought in to substitute for
the coherent voice lost with Cervantes's departure). He is also
instrumental in the development of the plot: it is he who is brings the
band into the mainstream of the Revolution, albeit for reasons of
personal greed (107-08), and it is he who introduces a romantic
element — doubtless a hangover from the tradition of novels written
in nineteenth-century Mexico — with Camila's infatuation for him.
His arrival on the scene in Chapter 5 of Part I is a pivotal moment in
the novel, and he soon becomes influential. He sows discord among
Macías's men, the first indication of disagreement with one of

Demetrio's decisions occurring when Cervantes is asked to take over the treatment of Demetrio's wound. The piqued Venancio then gives Demetrio an apposite warning: 'hay que saber que los curros son como la humedad, por dondequiera se filtran. Por los curros se ha perdido el fruto de las revoluciones' (99). Indeed, Cervantes soon insinuates himself into a powerful position as Macías's secretary and aide (many Mexican intellectuals attached themselves to revolutionary leaders in this fashion) and, like other interlopers who join the band, is a cause, or at least a catalyst, of degeneration. Azuela, then, makes Cervantes a representative of the opportunist intellectual. However, he was not content to leave him as a stereotype, but endowed him with a certain individuality, especially in the revised version of the novel.

Cervantes is clear-sighted in his ambition to make a fortune. At first he is horrified by Macías's men. When he realizes that the forces unleashed by the struggle against Díaz and Huerta are uncannily similar to the bandits he had described in his fawning newspaper articles — even though, as is made clear, when he was writing them he had thought that they were nothing but lies — he poses two of the key questions raised by *Los de abajo*: '¿Sería verdad lo que la prensa del gobierno y él mismo habían asegurado, que los llamados revolucionarios no eran sino bandidos agrupados ahora con un magnífico pretexto para saciar su sed de oro y de sangre? ¿Sería, pues, todo mentira lo que de ellos contaban los simpatizadores de la revolución?' (94). Yet his discovery that Macías's followers are brutal and ignorant bandits does not prevent his concluding that he was right to throw in his lot with them, for, despicable as they may be, they are going to be the victors, and wealth will be the reward for being on the winning side. Cervantes has a calculated approach to enriching himself: while his ignorant comrades loot impracticably large and showy objects which they are subsequently obliged to discard, he wants only portable booty: gems, gold, jewels and watches. Aware of the potential worthlessness of the paper money he embezzles, he is eager to transform it into objects which retain their value (167, 168). The final proof of his intelligence is his heeding the writing on the wall at the Aguascalientes Convention and his desertion immediately afterwards; some two months after the Convention, and far too quickly to be credible, he has used his looted fortune to finance his graduation as a doctor in the United States (181). Although largely a static character, Cervantes shows some signs of development. Nevertheless, despite what several critics maintain, Azuela makes it clear that he is not originally a sincere convert to the Revolution who is only gradually corrupted. He learns from his experiences and adapts to his environment, being taught a lesson by his initial treatment by the band; he curbs his ready tongue (99), learns to use the sort of Spanish his comrades understand (e.g. 'al buen sol hay que abrirle ventana', 155), and discovers how to insinuate himself by flattery and an appeal to his companions' baser instincts into an influential position (100, 110). His initial vilification by Macías's men (86) is followed by their ignoring him (104), and then, at last, accepting him as their advisor (108-09). He also becomes more shameless as the novel progresses: at first he disguises his motives as revolutionary idealism (107-09, 124); he is later willing to admit to Macías his desire for loot (142); and eventually he argues openly for self-interest (155-56).

Azuela also gives Cervantes a certain psychological depth. We have already seen that he lies to others; more interestingly, he deceives himself. There is some subtlety in the way the author ensures that the truth emerges from behind the false image which Cervantes projects and even tries to believe. For example, in Chapter 6 of Part I we share his thoughts about his behaviour during the ambush Macías had laid for the *federales* (among whom Cervantes was then serving), and his subsequent awakening to the plight of Mexico's poor. This account, which was introduced in the 1920 version of the novel, is narrated in what is now commonly known as *style indirect libre*, or free indirect style, a technique frequently employed by the nineteenth-century realists Azuela admired and much in evidence in *Los de abajo*. Rather than giving us a character's direct speech or thoughts indicated by inverted commas, this form of narration provides indirect discourse, but the fact that it is indirect is not marked by an introductory phrase like 'she thought that' or 'he remarked that'. We therefore have to be sufficiently attentive as readers to realize that the narrative is not coming direct from the omniscient narrator but is being filtered through a character's consciousness. We are usually alerted to this because we recognize that the style being used and the opinions voiced are those of a character rather than the ones we have come to associate with the omniscient narrator. Free indirect style summarizes or edits the character's speech or thoughts, as indirect discourse does, but presents that speech or those thoughts dramatically, as does direct discourse. It provides an insight into a character, and it can be used by authors to ironize that character. In the account of the ambush, we realize that the narration is being filtered through Cervantes's mind because we recognize his voice at its most cliché-ridden, the superficial elegance of his style suggesting that he is using language to mask, rather than reveal, the truth. But he overdoes it; he protests his innocence too much, even attempting to exonerate himself from the charge of cowardice by transferring to his horse the blame for his flight:

> Juraría, la mano puesta sobre un Santo Cristo, que cuando los soldados se echaron los máuseres a la cara, alguien con estentórea voz había clamado a sus espaldas: '¡Sálvese el que pueda!' Ello tan claro así que su mismo brioso y noble corcel, avezado a los combates, había vuelto grupas y de estampida no había querido detenerse sino a distancia donde ni el rumor de las balas se escuchaba. (88)

We recognize the sham he is attempting to believe for what it is, just as he tries to persuade himself that, after deserting the battle-field, he had merely been looking for shelter for the night, and yet inadvertently employs the word 'escondite' to describe it (89). All this suggests that Cervantes's protestations that his experiences with the *federales* led him to acquire a concern for the downtrodden are equally a mask for self-interest, a suggestion confirmed by the way he is persuaded to join the opposition to Huerta by three of his *federal* comrades. The first complains about the injustice of the *leva*, but the second and third — the ones who make a deep impression upon Cervantes — tell him that there is money to be made by going over to the revolutionaries (89-90).

More subtly, Cervantes persuades himself that his relationship with the young blonde girl he takes to Macías's drunken banquet is something more than that of an owner to an item of booty of which he intends to make sexual use (as a medical student with a strong instinct for self-preservation, he prudently avoids the syphilitic prostitutes to whom the other soldiers have recourse). When talking of her to his comrades he misleadingly refers to her as his *novia*, but it is a measure of his self-deceit that he also uses the same word when thinking about her (148). Cervantes's behaviour at the banquet suggests murkier depths to his character. He flaunts the ravishing adolescent before his comrades and is gratified to see that she excites Demetrio's lust (145), but when he later discovers that the foot which has forced its way suggestively between hers is not, as he had thought, Demetrio's but that of Margarito, he is furious (147). This is one of the very few times Cervantes shows any emotion other than greed, but, despite his anger on this occasion, there is no subsequent indication of his reaction to the girl's rape by Margarito. Indeed, Cervantes's motives in this scene appear particularly ambiguous. Perhaps he wishes his superior social status to be apparent to his leader after Demetrio has won fame at Zacatecas while he, Cervantes, has been hiding safely amid the ruined buildings; perhaps he wants to use Demetrio's desire for the girl as a means to reassert his ascendancy over him, because that ascendancy has been threatened by the irruption of La Pintada and Margarito into the band — we will remember that a result of his subsequent procurement of Camila for Demetrio is to diminish La Pintada's influence and, as a looter with a reputation for ferreting out the richest prizes (146), she is a potential rival to Cervantes; possibly he even sees a chance of profiting in some way from procuring a desirable sexual partner for Macías, as he will do in Chapter 7 of Part II, but this would scarcely be compatible, at least in the short term, with his own intention of enjoying the girl (148). Whatever Cervantes's motives, he has ambiguous feelings towards her: while he pretends to himself that she is his *novia*, he encourages Demetrio to behave to her in a way no respectable fiancé would permit. It is significant that although, by knocking Cervantes unconscious, Demetrio is the direct cause for the girl's having fallen into Margarito's hands, Cervantes never rebukes him for this, nor does it appear to affect their relationship in any way. The girl is abused and discarded, no further reference being made to her, and the whole affair illustrates Cervantes's callous disregard for others. For all their animality, the other characters are at least open about their sexual needs, and take direct action to satisfy them; Cervantes, on the other hand, disguises both his lust and his intention to use the girl. Macías, Margarito, and the common run of the revolutionaries normally make do with prostitutes and promiscuous camp-followers; they are not consequently as corrupting as Cervantes, for he is responsible for introducing the child into their midst, and therefore for her rape by the diseased and perverted Margarito. In a parallel fashion, it is again Cervantes who brings Camila into the band, and is thus indirectly to blame for her death at the hands of Margarito's companion, La Pintada.

Cervantes is the root of much of the evil in the book. In this he is not only an individual, but also a representative character, for Azuela implies through him that intellectuals, who should have given a responsible lead in the Revolution, channelling the energy of the uncouth masses towards positive ends, were exclusively concerned to enrich themselves and to further their own careers. Cervantes is educated, his perspective is less limited than that of his comrades, as Macías's aide he has his leader's ear, and his advice is respected (109, 174). He could have been a powerful force for good. Instead, he is too wrapped up in his own hypocritical speechifying to communicate with the ignorant soldiers, and his counsel is intended to manipulate others for his own unworthy ends (108-09, 155-56).

Macías and Cervantes

As I mentioned earlier, one method of characterization employed by Azuela in *Los de abajo* is comparison and contrast. This can be illustrated in the two characters examined above. The most obvious

contrast is that Demetrio is a rural Indian and Cervantes a city-bred
white: while Demetrio has 'mejillas cobrizas de indígena de pura
raza' (114), Azuela describes in some detail Cervantes's pink cheeks,
smooth white skin, and wavy blonde hair (102; although this
description may be idealized as it is possibly filtered through
Camila's consciousness). The irony of this description lies in
Cervantes's 'tierna expresión' (a phrase added to the revised version),
for it certainly does not reflect the inner man. We have already seen
that Azuela uses the physical description of the mass of the
revolutionaries to denote character; the very fact that the tenderness
seen in Cervantes's eyes is deceptive indicates his duplicity when
compared with his more straightforward comrades. His physical
appearance is also suggestive in a different way. Azuela writes from
within a society conditioned by *machista* attitudes, and for a readership which shares these attitudes. Demetrio's *machismo* is therefore
admirable, the percipient Solís, for one, being impressed by his
bravery at Zacatecas (132). Demetrio enjoys several women and
handles his horses with mastery. Cervantes, on the other hand, looks
effeminate, is likened to a doll (102), has no women, and cannot
even stay in the saddle (132); he himself claims that his horse
dominates him (88), and his planned sexual adventure with his
supposed *novia* ends up with his merely being invited to peep at her
and her rapist through a key-hole (149). Cervantes substitutes words
and intentions for action, and his lack of *machismo* may make him
an even more despicable figure for a contemporary Mexican reader,
rendering the contrast with Demetrio particularly striking.

While Demetrio develops and is, to some extent, treated
sympathetically — we have already noted that Azuela ensures that
the reader is left at the end of the novel with a predominantly
positive impression of him — Cervantes is largely static, his
characterization verges upon caricature, and the last we hear of him
is his attempt to trick a gullible comrade out of his loot (181-82).
Macías's inarticulateness, ignorance, and ingenuousness are
favourably contrasted with Cervantes's fluency, flattery, and
misdirected intelligence. The former's courageous participation in
military action is juxtaposed with the latter's cowardice and

prevarication when action is threatened. Cervantes is, admittedly, instrumental in Demetrio's joining the mainstream of the Revolution, but his role in this is merely that of a middle-man: he mouths the ideals claimed by some of the Revolution's leaders, but has no belief in them himself. His role as middle-man is most clearly symbolized by his association with women, for he is a pander who procures Camila for Demetrio and, unwittingly, the blonde girl for Margarito: 'pimp' is the word euphemistically omitted by Azuela from the revolutionaries' comments about Cervantes: 'Pa mí el tal curro no es más que un...', '¿Sabes lo que es ese curro?... ¡Palabra!... ¡Te digo que no más para eso lo trae el general!' (158). Demetrio may be brutal on occasion but his relationship with Camila demonstrates that he does at least have feelings: he also shows affection for his wife and child, for Cervantes and Anastasio, and he is capable of talking about his feelings when he confides to Cervantes his timidity with women (157). He is impulsive, his lack of premeditation suggesting a warmth, spontaneity, and unpredictability entirely lacking in Cervantes who has no close relationship with any other character in the novel and seems incapable of love or compassion (169). The difference can be illustrated by their contrasting attitudes to Camila: Demetrio admits that she is ugly, but is attracted by her gentleness and the sweetness of her voice (84, 91, 129); Cervantes thinks of her merely as a vulgar peasant, a monkey, who irritates him and whose voice puts his teeth on edge (94, 101). Finally, Demetrio's lack of desire for personal gain is highlighted by Cervantes's greed, Azuela possibly implying here something more disturbing. Demetrio is swept along by events, but during moments of inaction he has contact with, or looks back with nostalgia to, his past and the home he has left (105-07, 153, 165-66, 193-94). Cervantes has no family or home to tie him to the past; we know nothing of his family origins, and when his life before the Revolution is mentioned it is a source of acute embarrassment to him (125-26). Unlike his comrades who live from day to day, squandering all they steal (178), Cervantes looks to the future ('Hay que ver siempre adelante', 155), is correct in his predictions and is single-minded in his accumulation of wealth. Unlike Demetrio, he has clear ambitions, and he realizes them (94,

181-82). From the contrast between these two characters' attitudes to
the past and the future we draw the damning conclusion that it was
to the likes of Cervantes, the new men who became powerful once
the Revolution had been institutionalized, that the future of Mexico
was to belong.

The Women

Azuela contrasts Cervantes with Macías in order to characterize both
and also to pass an important judgement upon the Revolution, but
this technique of contrast or comparison is not limited to these two
characters. We have already seen that a comparison can be made
between Cervantes and La Pintada; one can similarly be drawn
between Cervantes and Margarito — both sycophantic outsiders who
hasten the decline of the band. Likewise, we are invited to compare
Demetrio favourably with most of his other followers, in particular
with Margarito, while he is compared with his *compadre* Anastasio
Montañés who shares many of his virtues. Cervantes is also
unfavourably contrasted with another intellectual, Solís. Camila, for
her part, is contrasted with both Cervantes and the other important
female character in the novel, La Pintada. Little psychological depth
is given to either woman, but this could be said to reflect the position
of women in the Revolution, who, in the main, played only a
supporting role as *soldaderas*, prostitutes, or the victims of what was
predominantly a struggle between men.

　　Although La Pintada may well be typical of some of the
footloose prostitutes who followed the armies during the Mexican
Revolution, Azuela avoids presenting her simply as a picturesque
type and endows her with a measure of individuality (*16*, p.87). She
is, of course, far from being the submissive woman of the *sierra* with
whom Macías feels at ease (165), and her very name draws attention
to her unnaturalness. A woman among men, she is more masculine
than feminine in her handshake (139), her drinking (155), swearing
(149, 172), indifference to danger (147), and even in her appearance
as a revolutionary — she does not maintain female decorum by
riding sidesaddle, but 'perniabierta' (151), at the same time a manly

and a suggestive posture, and carries the revolutionary's typical cartridge belt and revolver. She is sexually provocative, syphilitic, forthright in speech and impulsive in action, jealous, a liar, easily moved to laughter by trickery, cruelty and others' misfortunes, determined to have what she wants, and successful in achieving it (138-41). One of her roles in the novel is to corrupt the band: she does this both by the example she shows the soldiers, and by seducing their leader, who is so nonplussed by her brazenness, resolution and passion that he is incapable of ridding himself of her (157), is physically dominated by her (148), and eventually is unable to bring himself to execute her for the murder of Camila (172-73). It is she, like Margarito, who introduces the peasants to the worst excesses of the Revolution; she is a hardened revolutionary who had joined Villa's División del Norte at Tierra Blanca (146), presumably in November 1913, some eight months before the battle of Zacatecas after which she meets Macías. Her experiences have given her a simple philosophy:

> ¿Pos de dónde son ustedes? Si eso de que los soldados vayan a parar a los mesones es cosa que ya no se usa. ¿De dónde vienen? Llega uno a cualquier parte y no tiene más que escoger la casa que le cuadre y ésa agarra sin pedirle licencia a naiden. Entonces ¿pa quén jue la revolución? ¿Pa los catrines? Si ahora nosotros vamos a ser los meros catrines. (141)

It is remarkably similar to that of Cervantes (124), but, expressed in a language her comrades can comprehend, it is an immediately persuasive one. In a trice she is taking charge, giving orders, and leading by example. Soon the band can be described as 'La Pintada y sus compañeros' (142). She instructs them in looting and vandalism, and her habit of bringing her horse into human dwellings (146, 155) — a clear reference to the breakdown of civilized life during the Revolution — is immediately imitated by the band (159). She is, of course, a negative force in the novel and in Part II, which traces the decline of Macías's followers, their aimlessness and anarchy mirroring the fragmentation of the Revolution after the defeat of Huerta, she represents the corrosive influence of revolutionary experience upon Macías and his rural bandits of Jalisco. On occasion she may seem to show some sympathy for other women (150, 158), but Azuela leaves it ambiguous whether this concern is genuine or merely motivated by her jealousy of potential or actual rivals. Although not drawn in detail, La Pintada is a vivid character, and the impression she makes upon the reader is disproportionate to the infrequency and brevity of her appearances in the novel. In her unmanning of men and outswearing of troopers, her perspicacity, fearlessness, independence, decisiveness, and her ability to impose herself on that most male of institutions, an army, she could well prove an intriguing subject for feminist critics.

Camila, by contrast, is a shadowy figure, and it is worth remembering that, unlike La Pintada, she is not based on any living person. She is a type: the *serrana* of Azuela's native region (at one point he talks of her 'curiosidad de serrana' as if he considered it an inherent trait of all *serranas*: 93). She is plain and ignorant, lively and inquisitive, kind, gentle, ingenuous, sensitive, sincere, and submissive to those she loves. Azuela's claim that she was invented to suit the requirements of his plot or the novel's structure is enlightening (5, III, p.1086), for she is largely an unindividualized pawn both of the Revolution, in which she is caught up (the dead leaf associated with her, 111, is recalled later, 126, as an image of all those who are swept along by the gale of the Revolution), and of the author who uses her as a contrast to La Pintada and as evidence for the destruction wreaked by the Revolution upon all that is of value. This is why she is often placed against a background of tranquil Nature (110, 111, 163, 164) and is described in a positive image expressing her youth and vitality: 'Camila [...] con la ligereza del cervatillo [...]' (102). She will later be associated with the parallel image of a 'mariposita' (note again the affectionate diminutive) but, ominously, it is now a 'mariposita muerta' which is destroyed and discarded (111).

Other Characters

Most of the other characters in *Los de abajo* are only impressionisti-
cally sketched types. Margarito is, like La Pintada, a representative
of the pernicious influence of the Revolution upon Macías's followers in Part II, yet, although he appears sporadically in only half of
the novel, Azuela does give him enough individual traits to create a
lasting impression on the reader. Similarly, Margarito's fellow ex-
convict, Anastasio Montañés, who is sometimes directly contrasted
with him, is endowed with a certain life of his own.

Margarito is an ex-waiter who is resentful of those he once
served (160). One of his first actions in the book is to avenge on a
fellow waiter the indignities he had suffered himself in that job
(140), and one of the last images we have of him is his laughingly
shooting an ear off another waiter, and then wrecking a bar before
the eyes of the powerless barman (175). Azuela suggests that there is
no solidarity among such people; when they cease to be the
underdogs, their first impulse is to abuse the weak just as they
themselves had once been abused. Their philosophy is that so clearly
expressed by La Pintada. Margarito is a short man, and has a small
man's desire to humiliate and exploit those who fall into his hands
(170), especially if they are even smaller than he is (176). He is
introduced by Anastasio as 'reteacabado' (crafty) (138), and the
implications of this description are seen when he cunningly steals the
key to the bedroom in which Cervantes's blonde girl is locked, rapes
her, and is again approvingly described, this time by La Pintada, as
'[el] hombre más acabado' (149). He has a reputation as a joker, a
man who can claim that he will even make Demetrio laugh after
Camila's death. But his laughter, like that of La Pintada and the mass
of the soldiers who are in their thrall, is provoked by cruelty, anarchy
and the humiliation of others. It is to Demetrio's credit that he is not
amused (163, 174-75). A flatterer like Cervantes, with whom his
blue eyes and blonde hair (traditionally sinister features in Mexican
literature) are tacitly compared, he is another white city-dweller who
leads astray the peasant band. While an Indian like Demetrio is
impassive, Margarito is volatile (140), quick-tongued (139), disloyal

(172-73) and, as we saw previously, sadistic. Like La Pintada, he exerts a strong influence over the band, his judgement being respected (159), his orders obeyed (168), and his example followed or, at least, seldom challenged (168). Although his behaviour runs contrary to Macías's expressed wishes and is eventually denounced by Margarito's erstwhile friend Anastasio, Demetrio does nothing to curb him, and Azuela dispatches him from the novel when, at the end of Part II, he has served his purpose (181).

Anastasio typifies Azuela's opinion of the *rancheros* of Jalisco as good-hearted braggarts. He claims to have a body full of lead, to know all there is to know about women, to be a fearless *macho*, to be above the common mass of the revolutionaries' gambling and swearing, to be respected, and to enjoy prosperity as a smallholder (78, 91, 103, 129, 131). This complacency and his linguistic idiosyncrasies ('¿A que no me lo crees?', etc.: 78, 103, 131) make him fair game for La Codorniz's ready wit (131). His black beard reveals that he is not an Indian, and his gentle eyes suggest impassivity and indifference to the cruelty that he witnesses and in which he participates. He is Demetrio's *compadre*, acting as his right-hand man, tending him when wounded, rescuing him when in danger, and curbing him when drunk (78, 79, 83, 84, 87, 98, 118, 148). He is ignorant, uncouth, and superstitious, being mocked not only by the other characters for his boastfulness but also, on occasion, by the author for his rusticity (145, 146), yet he offers Demetrio sensible advice, can be gentle, and is outraged by Margarito's excesses (98, 93, 170). Although certainly not idealized, for he will kill and loot like the next man, he possesses a kind of honesty and says what he thinks; indeed, he often asks, in his ingenuous and slow-witted way, key questions about the Revolution (109, 131, 182, 190-91, 192). It is significant that he plays a substantial role in Part I, but is eclipsed by La Pintada and Margarito in Part II; he is displaced by the forces of anarchy, and tricked by the sharper *parvenus* (187), but his straightforwardness and loyalty are favourably contrasted with their duplicity and insubordination. He is, then, largely a type, but is not treated unsympathetically: he is the first to join Demetrio, he is his loyal comrade throughout, and he dies alongside his *compadre* at the end of the novel, Demetrio shedding tears at his death (196). Like Demetrio, he seems to have little desire to profit from the Revolution. He is just one of its uncomprehending victims; an example, perhaps, of the sort of men who, if they had been guided by right-minded intellectuals, could have saved Mexico from what Azuela saw as the tragic outcome of the conflict.

The intellectuals are, of course, represented by Cervantes, Solís and Valderrama. Cervantes, as we have seen, is a cynic who mouths idealistic phrases. Solís, on the other hand, is a genuine idealist, but one who has been disillusioned by his experiences as Natera's adjutant. He appears briefly (in the main in Chapters 18 and 21 of Part I) and is only lightly sketched. He is a functional character who serves both to confirm, by contrast, the reader's poor opinion of Cervantes, and also to utter the most important statements in the novel. His disillusion appears to be proportional to his exaggerated optimism at the outset of the Revolution: 'Yo pensé una florida pradera al remate de un camino... Y me encontré un pantano' (125), a quotation which Azuela borrowed from one of his own short stories and added to the 1920 version of the novel (5, II, p.1074). It is possible that Azuela here hints at Solís's own shortcomings: he is not an entirely admirable character acting unequivocally as a spokesman for the author despite the fact that Azuela identifies with him on one occasion (5, III, p.1081): although he is aware of the emptiness of the rhetoric used by intellectuals during the Revolution (129-30), he is also guilty of distorting the truth for the ignorant fighters (126), and though he dies pointlessly trying to impress Cervantes (135), his personal courage is left in some doubt (132-33). As we have seen, he bases his judgement of the Revolution exclusively on his observation of his comrades, and believes that the fundamental flaw in the Revolution is a moral, human one: 'hay hombres que no son sino pura hiel... Y esa hiel va cayendo gota a gota en el alma, y todo lo amarga, todo lo envenena. Entusiasmo, esperanzas, ideales, alegrías..., ¡nada!' (125). Like Azuela, he does not conceive of the Revolution as a wider process which, however distasteful in immediate detail, may achieve something positive in the long term. Azuela shares with Solís an ambiguous fascination with and detestation of violence (135), yet, given Solís's shortcomings, it is imprudent to consider him unambiguously, as most critics have done, as nothing but a spokesman for the author.

Valderrama, introduced for the first time in the 1920 version of *Los de abajo*, is similarly pressed into service to utter general statements about the Revolution. After Cervantes's disappearance, the author requires a coherent voice, and thus introduces Valderrama who is brought into and dispatched from the novel in a peremptory manner. By making the intellectual who replaces Cervantes an alcoholic suffering from more than a touch of madness, Azuela was possibly making a comment about the Revolution, for this degenerate figure parallels the decline of Macías's band in the final Part of the novel and, in turn, mirrors what, in Azuela's view, was the decline of the Revolution after the Aguascalientes Convention. However, it is equally possible that the author merely wished to introduce into his novel a figure modelled on his great friend José Becerra, to whom he dedicated the revised 1920 edition. The description he gives elsewhere of Becerra reveals close similarities between model and character: Becerra was an old-fashioned and wildly eccentric romantic poet, an alcoholic, and — oddly enough for an officer who rode with the *villistas* — incapable of countenancing any violence to man or beast (5, III, pp.797-807). These characteristics are faithfully reproduced in Valderrama. It seems that Azuela even borrowed directly from Becerra for Valderrama's apocalyptic speech paralleling that of Solís in Chapter 18 of Part I (28, p.106): the Revolution is a beautiful natural cataclysm beyond Man's control: '¿Villa?... ¿Obregón?... ¿Carranza?... ¡X... Y... Z...! ¿Qué se me da a mí?... ¡Amo la Revolución como amo al volcán que irrumpe! ¡Al volcán porque es volcán; a la Revolución porque es Revolución!' (186-87), a statement again transferred from an earlier story to the 1920 version of the novel (see 5, II, p.1073). Yet Valderrama is an unsatisfactory character, on the one hand because the reader unfamiliar with the model is not provided with a convincing enough portrait to allow the character to stand in his own right, on the other because he is so obviously wheeled in and out of the novel to make tendentious comments. Although closely based on a real and colourful person, Valderrama remains a functional and commonplace character — the madman who utters profound truths.

The minor figures in *Los de abajo* are portrayed in thumb-nail sketches and are normally distinguished merely by one or two characteristics. Thus, for example, La Codorniz is a womanizer and a joker, employing comic language and being chosen to dress up ludicrously as a priest. Such traits differentiate the minor characters from each other as do the hints provided of their origins and their reasons for joining the Revolution (*22*, pp.1008-09). In this they represent a cross-section of the humbler participants in the turmoil. They are largely static types seen against a background of social and historical circumstances which enable them to indulge their particular vices unrestrained. However, such sketchiness does not preclude vividness, nor is it necessarily a weakness in the novel. Through these figures Azuela portrays the mass of common revolutionaries, and it is not surprising that they should be flat characters against whom the more rounded characters emerge. Indeed, it could be argued that their very lack of detailed characterization mirrors not only the way the mass of anonymous fighters must be perceived by anybody involved in a chaotic revolution, but also how the Mexican Revolution reduced the individual humanity of its participants.

In this chapter I have dwelled at some length upon character and characterization because these are aspects of the novel which have been frequently criticized. Clearly, *Los de abajo* is far from being a psychological study; Azuela offers no insights into most of his creatures' thoughts and, in the main, his figures are portrayed in a behaviouristic manner and in a dynamic narrative which has no time for analysis. Nevertheless, some of them do have depth, and Azuela is skilled in the rapid creation of vivid characters through speech and facial expression. He was aware that in the Revolution he was dealing with a new experience and that he had to forge a new medium to express it. One of his innovatory techniques for a realist portrayal of ordinary Mexicans was his dramatic characterization which relied upon the nuances and variations of the spoken word, rather as a play script does, tone and stylistic idiosyncrasies often being the only indication of a speaker's identity. Indeed, dialogue largely replaces the lengthy description traditionally found in realist novels. Azuela uses a range of registers of oral language to distinguish educated speakers from the uneducated, and the rural from the urban. Characters are individualized and placed on a geographical and social map by the variety of Mexican Spanish they speak, and this method of characterization was further developed in the 1920 version of the novel (*4*, pp.258-60). Nevertheless, as we have seen, Azuela's characterization also owes much to the nineteenth-century European writers he so admired. Real people are closely observed and such observation is employed in the creation of credible characters who are often treated in an apparently objective manner; however, this portrayal of character is coloured by the author's pessimistic, deterministic vision and thus serves to convey a personal view of the Revolution. We shall see in the next chapter that the structure of *Los de abajo* fulfils the same purpose.

4. Structure

Most critics who discuss the structure of *Los de abajo* refer, on the one hand, to Azuela's own statement that the novel is 'una serie de cuadros y escenas de la revolución constitucionalista, débilmente atados por un hilo novelesco' (*5*, III, p.1078), and, on the other, to the novel's obvious circularity, Macías being killed in the very canyon in which he had laid his first ambush. There is some discrepancy between the recognition that Azuela gave his work a circular framework and the assertion that it has a haphazard structure. This discrepancy has given rise to considerable critical debate (e.g. *12*, p.229; *18*, p.48; *22*; *25*; *34*). Some writers have maintained that, as the early version of the novel was written under great pressure, it is misguided to look for a carefully wrought structure in it, but while this may well be true of the 1915 version, it need not be so of the 1920 edition which was revised at leisure. Others, particularly Marxist critics such as Dessau, have claimed that, while Part I is ordered, Part II becomes increasingly incoherent, a feature of the novel they attribute to Azuela's disillusion at the failure of *maderismo* and particularly at the way the Revolution developed after the battle of Zacatecas. They contend that, as a bourgeois liberal, Azuela was incapable of understanding fully the revolutionary process and that his bewilderment resulted in the fragmentary and incoherent structure of *Los de abajo* after the capture of Zacatecas, an event which takes place at the end of Part I (*12*, pp.223, 229). However, the reader should be aware that Dessau's comments concerning the lack of organization in Part II of the novel are based upon a particular historical analysis of the Revolution: that it was a clear process of class struggle in which the exploited rose up against their exploiters. Different conclusions about the structure of Part II in particular and of *Los de abajo* as a whole can be reached if

a more liberal interpretation of historical events is adopted. I should
not go as far as to claim that Azuela patterns the novel's narrative
structure rigorously, but even a cursory examination of the way the
novel is put together does suggest that he took some care over this
aspect of his work. For example, he controls the pace of his revised
1920 version to reach a climax at the end of the book: Part I contains
twenty-one chapters, Part II fourteen, and Part III seven. Closer
study reveals numerous symmetries and a coherent development.
Structure often plays an active part in carrying the message of a
work rather than merely being an empty vessel into which content is
poured, and therefore some general conclusions about the meaning
or message of *Los de abajo* may legitimately be drawn from an
examination of the novel's construction. As it is the structure of Part
II that has been subjected to particular censure, I shall examine it in
isolation before turning to the organization of the novel as a whole.

The Structure of Part II

In the final chapter of Part I, Solís pronounces an aphoristic
judgement upon the genetic deficiencies of the Mexican race, as he
calls it, Azuela here reflecting the positivist ideas common in
Porfirian Mexico and in the works of some of his favourite French
authors. Solís sums up 'la psicología de nuestra raza, condensada en
dos palabras: ¡robar, matar!' (135). Didactic works frequently
introduce an aphorism and then employ particular examples to
support the validity of the generalized proposition. In the case of *Los
de abajo*, Solís's statement is illustrated by the whole of Part II, and
the structure of this section of the novel is determined to some extent
by it. Chapter 1 is probably set in Fresnillo during the looting of that
town by the revolutionaries. As they sit drinking in a restaurant they
begin to boast about the killing they have engaged in, each death
being more gratuitous than the last:

> — Yo maté dos coroneles — clama con voz ríspida y
> gutural un sujeto pequeño y gordo [...].

> — Yo en Torreón, maté a una vieja que no quiso venderme un plato de enchiladas. [...]

> — Yo maté a un tendajonero en el Parral porque me metió en un cambio dos billetes de Huerta [...].

> — Yo, en Chihuahua, maté a un tío porque me lo topaba siempre en la mesma mesa y a la mesma hora, cuando yo iba a almorzar [...].

> — ¡Hum!... Yo maté... (137, 140)

The narrator then intervenes sententiously to add the statement, 'El tema es inagotable' (140). The last chapter of Part II illustrates the other inherent defect attributed to Mexicans by Solís: the impulse to rob. Macías's band is travelling by train to the Aguascalientes Convention when an old woman appeals to them for alms, astutely claiming to have been robbed of her life savings by a well-dressed gentleman. She meets with a sympathetic response and the conversation soon turns to the subject of theft:

> — [...] La purita verdá es que yo he robao [...].

> —¡Hum, pa las máquinas de coser que yo me robé en México! [...]

> — Yo me robé en Zacatecas unos caballos tan finos [...].
> Lo malo fue que mis caballos le cuadraron a mi general Limón y él me los robó a mí. [...]

> — [...] Yo también he robado [...]. (178)

The narrator again steps in with, 'El tema del "yo robé", aunque parece inagotable [...]' (178). The similarity of these two passages, which are to be found at the beginning and end of Part II, enables us to see this Part — which deals in the main with looting and killing — as a confirmation of Solís's damning judgement about Mexicans. Far from being incoherent, as Dessau claims, this Part of the novel appears to have been structured to convey a clear message.

There is a similar balance between the second and penultimate chapters of Part II where the revolutionary band is described in the most unfavourable of lights as a threat to civilized life. In Chapter 2, La Pintada, who has only recently joined the group, leads the search for booty in an abandoned mansion. Azuela concentrates upon the fighters' ignorant destruction of beautiful objects culminating in the ripping apart by a young, syphilitic prostitute of a copy of the *Divine Comedy* — not a gratuitous detail, for not only does Dante's work represent a pillar of universal culture being defiled by the rabble, but the scene in which it is destroyed conjures up a vision of the particular Hell of the Revolution. It is, of course, understandable that a writer like Azuela should have been outraged by such behaviour; it is equally understandable that illiterate peasants should have set little store by a high culture from which they were excluded. It is no coincidence that, in the balancing penultimate chapter, it is La Pintada's companion, Margarito, who has now become the dominant force in the group. He shoots up a restaurant in Lagos and later endangers the life of an innocent shopkeeper who is going about his own business. Azuela's decision to set such thuggery in his home town adds a further note of indignation at the violation of what he would consider decent values. The scenes of anarchy orchestrated by these two characters are carefully counterpoised.

It would be an exaggeration to claim that Azuela neatly balances chapter against chapter throughout Part II; his structure is not that systematic. But the balance of the first two and last two chapters, and the general development of this Part, refute the assertion that it is merely the result of the arbitrary stringing together of episodes. Indeed, Part II parallels Part I by setting the limited and private concerns of Macías and his band against the important historical events of the Revolution. In Part I the band is formed for parochial reasons (the persecution of Macías by Don Mónico and the *federales*, etc.), yet is sucked into major events at Zacatecas because of Cervantes's advice. In Part II there is a similar progression: one of the major events of the Part is the band's parochial concern to return to Moyahua in order to settle their score with Don Mónico, but Macías is drawn back into the mainstream of the Revolution by a summons to attend the Aguascalientes Convention. Nor is Part II structured only around the alternation of the parochial and the national; it also makes play with an alternation of aimless and purposeful activity. Thus the aimless looting of a town after the capture of Zacatecas (Chapters 1-4) is followed by the purposeful return to Moyahua (Chapters 5-7); the aimless wandering in a vain attempt to locate *orozquistas* (Chapters 8-11) is followed by the purposeful journey to Aguascalientes (Chapters 12-14). It also chronicles a gradual process of degeneration; there is here a definite development rather than a simple accumulation of unrelated episodes, as Part II witnesses the growing dominance over the band of the values of La Pintada and Margarito who first appear in the initial chapter of the Part and have disappeared by the beginning of Part III.

The most graphic example of the group's degeneration is the murder of Camila. She is the only character to plead for an end to gratuitous cruelty and she is killed by La Pintada. So powerful is the latter's influence, however, that Macías is unable to execute her as a punishment for the murder and she goes free. There is a bitter irony in his indecision: he had previously, when drunk, tried to kill La Pintada for preventing him from raping a girl he did not know (148); he now makes no attempt to punish her for murdering a girl of whom he is genuinely fond. Similarly, in Part II, Macías's previous reluctance to take advantage of the defenceless peasants in the villages they encounter (110) and his opposition to looting in his native region (155) disappear, and he will eventually sanction the theft of the only sustenance of the family of a poor widower (169). It is Margarito who is a prime mover of the cruelty shown to the poor by Macías's band, but the degeneration depicted in this Part is epitomized by Cervantes's open declaration to Macías that their aim should be to make a quick profit from the Revolution and then leave Mexico. Cervantes ceases even to pretend to be fighting for any ideals, and Azuela highlights his brazenness by paralleling his cynical '¿Qué causa defenderíamos ahora?' (156) with the honest question Demetrio posed him on their first meeting: '¿Pos cuál causa defendemos nosotros?' (87).

These examples indicate that Part II of the novel possesses a measure of thematic unity and is structured with a particular purpose in view. However, it is true that it does appear, on a first reading, to be unstructured and fragmentary. Indeed, the whole book is built on a series of major and minor climaxes which occur at the ends of chapters and tend to make the novel seem disjointed but which successfully increase the tension (e.g. at the end of Chapter 3 of Part I we are left in doubt whether Macías has been killed by the *federales*; at the end of Chapter 5 we do not know whether Cervantes will be executed). Sometimes the discontinuity of the narrative realistically mirrors the discontinuity of experience as, for example, when the gap between Chapters 3 and 4 of Part II conveys how several hours are a blank for Cervantes after he had been knocked unconscious by Macías. These particular cases of discontinuity in the narrative are not arbitrary but have an artistic purpose; likewise, it is difficult to agree with those critics who maintain that the overall impression of incoherence and fragmentation is merely the result of Azuela's ceasing to understand a coherent revolutionary process. Macías's burning of Don Mónico's house closes the sequence of personal persecution and vengeance which was opened at the very beginning of the novel. This is the only series of events which Macías is capable of understanding fully, so it is therefore only natural that he and his band should be confused by all that follows and that the novel's structure should reflect their bewilderment. Such confusion is paralleled by the organization of Part II after the scene of Macías's revenge on Don Mónico, for it appears particularly aimless as the band wanders hither and thither looting and killing (they ride from Moyahua to Tepatitlán, back to Cuquío and then return to Tepatitlán). In the apparently episodic nature of much of Part II, Azuela encapsulates the revolutionaries' bewilderment during much of the fighting, and the aimlessness which was a particular characteristic of the *villista* forces operating in the *sierras*. The structure also embodies Azuela's disillusion with a Revolution which he believed to have been stripped of any purpose or ideal. It can be argued that this view was borne out by events and that his novel accurately reflects the course taken by the Revolution. Part I deals with the linear development of a small, isolated band's activities as it moves from haphazard skirmishes into the mainstream of the Revolution, a development that parallels the unfolding of the Mexican Revolution up to the storming of Zacatecas in June 1914. The fall of that city is considered by some historians to be the climax of the Revolution as it was the result of the struggle of the combined revolutionary forces against Huerta and the *federales* who represented Porfirian Mexico. Azuela's placing of the battle for Zacatecas at the mid-point of the novel (i.e. after twenty-one chapters) is not fortuitous. As we have seen, after the capture of that city, the revolutionaries fell out among themselves. This disintegration of the Revolution is faithfully reflected by Macías's confusion which is, in turn, paralleled by the apparently aimless structure of Part II of *Los de abajo*.

Part II of *Los de abajo* is not simply a series of loosely-linked episodes. Rather, it can be seen on closer scrutiny both to possess a certain roundness (as do several of its constituent chapters), balance, and development which are esthetically satisfying, and to pass a judgement on the Revolution. Nevertheless, it appears at first to be chaotic, and this apparent chaos reflects a legitimate interpretation of historical events.

The Structure of the Three Parts

Several of the features identified in the structure of Part II have their parallels in the organization of the novel as a whole. Among the techniques employed to give the work a certain unity is the use of parallelism between and within the various Parts in the pattern of events, characters, repeated phrases, leitmotifs, themes, and descriptions. Let us take a few examples to illustrate various types of parallelism. Parts I and II follow a similar pattern of events. Each contains an extensive sequence during which Macías's band is static — in Camila's village in Part I and in the looted town in Part II. This static sequence then gives way to movement in both Parts. Into village and town alike come characters from the outside who disrupt and corrupt: in Part I the outsider is Luis Cervantes; in Part II the

outsiders are Margarito and La Pintada. In the first chapter of Part I
Macías's domestic peace is shattered by a Federal soldier who claims
to have known him in the Penetenciaría de Escobedo; in the first
chapter of Part II, Macías's band is similarly disrupted by the introduction of Margarito who had known Anastasio Montañés in the
same prison. At the beginning of Part I, the band sets out from its
native region; in Part II it goes back there, only to leave again; in
Part III it returns home definitively.

There are three significant deaths and three survivals, one in
each Part: at the end of Part I, Solís, the disillusioned idealist, is
killed but the cynical Cervantes, who was inadvertently the cause of
his death, survives. Near the end of Part II, Camila is killed, yet her
murderess survives. At the end of Part III, Macías himself is killed,
but the survival of Cervantes is ironically emphasized in the first
chapter of that Part. In a similar way, Pancracio is associated with
sordid killing in each Part. In Part I he kills the brother of a villager
who helped Macías to defeat an enemy garrison; in Part II he gratu-
itously murders a sacristan; in Part III we hear that he has killed a
companion, and has himself been killed in a brawl. In Part I Macías's
house is burnt down; in Part II he burns down that of Don Mónico.
In Part I the *federales* are accused of a series of crimes; in Part II
these same crimes are committed by Macías's band. The ambush of
the *federales* by Macías in Part I is paralleled by that of Macías
himself in Part III; not only do both actions take place in the same
canyon, but they also have in common many descriptive details. In
Part I Camila falls in love with Cervantes, but he later introduces her
into the band to become Macías's mistress; in Part II Cervantes
introduces a second girl, the unnamed and terrified fourteen-year-
old, who will be abused by Margarito. In Part I the dark-skinned and
ugly Camila is used somewhat unsubtly to represent the goodness
and innocence of the simple Mexican peasant women of the *sierras*.
In Part II the blonde girl seems to represent the white city-dwelling
middle classes. Her purity is carefully stressed by the author: 'su piel
era fresca y suave como un pétalo de rosa' (145), and 'la chiquilla de
grandes ojos azules y semblante de virgen' (150). A filthy rag is
symbolically thrown over her shoulders after she has been raped by

Margarito — after, that is, she has had contact with the revolutionaries who sully her idealized beauty just as the ideals of the *maderistas* were defiled by the Revolution. Cervantes is the cause of the abasement of both girls: the intellectual is instrumental in the betrayal of both the peasantry and the middle classes as well as of the original ideals of the Revolution.

Leitmotifs — such as that of Macías's remembering his wife or Camila at moments of disillusion (128, 153, 165, 188) and a growing awareness of the inevitability of his fate (165, 194) — and even entire phrases echo each other from Part to Part and thus endow the novel with a certain unity (e.g. 156 and 180, 165 and 191). Certain themes are also constantly echoed throughout the novel. In all three Parts the Revolution gathers its own irresistible momentum; in each there is a statement which indicates both this and the fact that, despite the enormous amount of energy expended, the hectic action of revolution achieves nothing. Near the end of Part I, Solís points to this futile momentum: 'La revolución es el huracán, y el hombre que se entrega a ella no es ya el hombre, es la miserable hoja seca arrebatada por el vendaval' (126). This pessimistic and positivist image of the dry leaf at the mercy of an uncontrollable — and, indeed, cyclical — wind is one which recalls an earlier passage in the novel where such a leaf falls at the feet of Camila who will herself be swept up and destroyed by the violence of the Revolution (111). At the end of Part II, we again witness the inexorability of the Revolution when Natera cheerfully informs the perplexed Macías, '¡Cierto como hay Dios, compañero; sigue la bola!' (180), and at the end of Part III there is the oft-quoted statement uttered by Macías in an attempt to explain to his wife why he has to continue to fight: he throws a stone into a canyon and remarks, 'Mira esa piedra cómo ya no se para' (195).

Other recurrent elements which endow the three Parts with unity range from parallel descriptive passages (117 and 192; 114, 150, and 195; 77, 133, and 150) to more ambiguous scenes such as those which suggest the beauty of violence and which reflect a certain ambivalence in Azuela's view of the Revolution. In the thick of battle at the end of Part I Solís cries, '¡Qué hermosa es la

Revolución, aun en su misma barbarie!' (135), and Valderrama echoes this anarchic attraction in Part III, '¡Amo la Revolución como amo al volcán que irrumpe! ¡Al volcán porque es volcán; a la Revolución porque es Revolución!' (187). As so often in *Los de abajo*, violence is both repugnant and fascinating to Azuela, and this is nowhere clearer than in the carefully-wrought depiction of men and horses galloping away from a massacre (161), the beautiful picture of two cocks fighting to the death (188), and the descriptions of Nature in the last chapter of the novel. Much of Azuela's writing condemns the waste and brutality of a Revolution which, in his opinion, unleashed a wave of barbarism and anarchy upon his country, and which resulted in bloodshed, wanton destruction, and the mere substitution of the *caciques* he so despised by a new class of opportunists rather than being the process of moral regeneration which he believed necessary (5, III, p.666). Yet Azuela also saw that the Revolution meant freedom and an awakening for the exploited and, although he portrays some of his peasant characters in *Los de abajo* as uncouth thugs, he does show admiration for their spontaneous heroism and vibrancy, a genuine sympathy for the downtrodden, and the need to change the social order which oppresses them.

Some critics believe that Azuela's ambivalent view of the Revolution resulted from a conflict between his sympathy for the professed aim of the Revolution — to better the lot of the poor — and his deterministic conviction that mankind was doomed to be divided into exploiters and exploited, revolutions being fated always to fail (32, pp.88-89). Elsewhere, however, he seems to imply that, if this particular revolution did not realize its reforming potential, it was not because revolutions are all bound to fail, and there is even the hope that 'los de abajo' will eventually realize a just society (10, pp.17-18; 6, pp.308-09). Others maintain that ambivalence was the result of a bourgeois's incomprehension of the Revolution. Whatever its origins, Azuela's ambivalent view can be discerned in the final scene of the novel. By this point the most sadistic and corrupting members of the band (Pancracio, El Manteca, La Pintada, Margarito, and Cervantes) have disappeared, and the beautiful natural setting cleansed by rain suggests a more positive view of the rural revolu-

tionaries than we have seen in much that precedes it. Indeed, the way
in which he chooses to set the slaughter of Macías's band against the
incongruous background of Nature in its gayest of moods encapsulates Azuela's ambivalent view. The death of Macías amid the beauty
of Nature could imply, on the one hand, that the honest *ranchero* is
too noble to survive in a Revolution which has been hijacked by
opportunists and even that he is purified in death — 'Macías, con los
ojos fijos para siempre, sigue apuntando' (197), continuing, that is, to
show the way to a better future but also pointing an accusing finger
at those who have corrupted the Revolution (and the possible
implication of fruitfulness contained in the image 'los hombres de
Demetrio caen como espigas cortadas por la hoz' (196) supports a
positive interpretation). The description of Nature also reflects
Azuela's view of the beauty of the original ideals of a Revolution
which is said by Valderrama to have begun near the place where
Macías dies. On the other hand, a more negative interpretation can
be given to the beautiful description of Nature at the end of the
novel. At this, the lowest ebb of the band's fortunes, Nature appears
indifferent to the fate of puny men, its permanence being contrasted
with the transience of the individual: as Demetrio is killed, 'Las
cigarras entonan su canto imperturbable y misterioso; las palomas
cantan con dulzura en las rinconadas de las rocas; ramonean
apaciblemente las vacas' (196). Similarly, Nature had previously
mocked the revolutionaries' plight and had dwarfed them (113, 182).
This final scene of the novel highlights how a fundamentally decent
man has been caught up by forces and historical events as irresistible
as a natural cataclysm — the countryside described has been formed
by violent natural convulsions (197) — and has been doomed to die
having achieved nothing.

These examples indicate that the book possesses unity even if
a certain ambiguity underlies it. The overall development, and the
implications of this development, add to this coherence. The work is
certainly episodic; it is based upon a series of journeys and this gives
the impression of a loose structure where a cumulative effect is
created by linking together various adventures in a linear manner.
However, although apparently loosely connected, no episode is

redundant, and they combine to trace a general development which reflects the author's perception of the lack of ideals among the participants of the Revolution, the degeneration of some of the fighters, and the opportunism of others. This process of degeneration has already been identified as a key element of the structure of Part II. I shall now examine some examples of this process throughout the whole novel.

Macías's gradual loss of scruple about robbery from the poor — a point to which I referred as a feature of Part II — is developed in all three Parts. In Part I he promises the inhabitants of Camila's village that after the Revolution he will remember their kindness (112); he is also anxious to avoid alienating them as the *federales* had done by their thefts and abductions (110). However, when his men join the main revolutionary forces for the attack on Zacatecas, they witness the indiscriminate looting of even the poorest dwellings by those troops (127). In Part II, although his own forces loot Moyahua and terrify the inhabitants (151, 155), Macías is anxious to avoid giving the impression, at least in his own native region, that profit is his motive for fighting (155), even though he may not be averse to allowing his troops to rob the poor elsewhere (169). In Part III Azuela again returns to this theme and depicts the band now attempting to loot the villages of their own *sierra*. This degeneration is paralleled by the reception given to the revolutionaries in the villages through which they pass. In Part I they are well fed and cared for by the poor (84). In Part II, when the column arrives in Moyahua, the poor now hide from them (150, 159), but are not unwilling to profit from the presence of Macías's men in order to loot the homes of the rich (153-54). In Part III Macías's men encounter only fear and hostility from the poor, even of their native region, who give them no food and who mock their humiliation (183-84), and the revolutionaries persecute even the *serranos* of their home area (183). This progressive loss of popular support due to the soldiers' excesses is pointed up by Anastasio Montañés's nostalgic thoughts near the end of the novel (192). A similar development is seen in the growth of Macías's band. As it increases in numbers it recruits members from outside the Juchipila region who introduce dissension and usurp power from Macías for their own ends. Cervantes does this in Part I where he begins to influence Macías's decisions and persuades him to recruit prisoners (109). In Part II the influence is more brutal when, as I have shown, La Pintada and Margarito become the dominant forces and threaten the group's unity by internal strife and indiscipline. In Part III ex-*federales* have become officers and even conceal information from Macías and some of the veteran members of the band (187).

Just as the wanderings of the group are increasingly purpose-less — they engage in no real battle after the capture of Zacatecas — so does the group itself begin to disintegrate: by the beginning of Part III we know that La Pintada has left and that Margarito, Pancracio and El Manteca are dead. Subsequently, even the faithful Anastasio momentarily becomes critical of Macías's leadership (190-91), and Solís's prophecy of Part I, Chapter 18 is fulfilled: the Revolution is betrayed and the only options for the revolutionaries are to degenerate into simple banditry, as do Macías's men, or to desert, as do Cervantes and Valderrama.

A final example of such a loss of purpose can be seen in the band's growing aimlessness. I have already discussed this with regard to Parts I and II, but it is in Part III that Azuela drives home his point. The troops range wide — we hear that they have been as far afield as Tepic in the province of Nayarit (192) — and, until they return to Juchipila, the location of the action remains vague. The lack of purpose in their wanderings is stressed: 'Su marcha por los cañones era ahora la marcha de un ciego sin lazarillo; se sentía ya la amargura del éxodo' (189). This decline, in which movement becomes an end in itself, just as fighting has become for Macías's men (182), clearly illustrates Azuela's thesis that the original *maderista* ideals of the Revolution have been lost. Azuela makes sure that his reader does not miss the point: when the ragged and demoralized revolutionaries return to Juchipila, Valderrama apostro-phizes the town, praising it as the cradle of the *maderista* Revolution, but his speech is cynically deflated by an ex-*federal* officer, and Valderrama abandons his lament in order to beg a drink of tequila (190). Nor do the intellectuals give disinterested guidance:

in Part I Cervantes had provided Macías's men with a reason for fighting, even if he did not believe in his own explanations (108-09, 124). In Part II he discloses his real materialistic motives for supporting the Revolution (156). In Part III, with Cervantes's disappearance, the revolutionaries are at a loss to know why the struggle is still going on, and their questions about the purpose of the continual blood-letting go unanswered (182).

Los de abajo, then, possesses a certain overall unity created through the use of balance, the fulfilment of prophecy, constant thematic concerns and repeated echoes of actions and descriptions. While its structure is episodic, the novel is not arbitrarily ordered, but, rather, progressively develops a thesis. This thesis provides a further explanation for Azuela's portrayal of events such as the battle of Zacatecas, the Aguascalientes Convention and Villa's defeat at Celaya. They were three key episodes in the Revolution and marked three separate phases of the struggle; one is seen in each Part of the novel. I have already suggested that his realist method led him to concentrate on the humdrum rather than the heroic and to de-centre history as some of his nineteenth-century predecessors had done (see above, pp.39-40), but his deliberately off-hand treatment of the major historical events of the Revolution also has the purpose of preventing any note of optimism from creeping into the novel. Thus, not only are these famous events referred to obliquely, but the highest point of the Revolution in Azuela's view, the capture of Zacatecas from the *federales*, is deflated by its ironic juxtaposition with the death of Solís and the sordid looting depicted at the beginning of Part II.

I have argued that not only Part II, but also the other Parts, possess an esthetically pleasing, though elusive, unity, and that the structure conveys a message. If these conclusions are accepted, we still have to ask why, in spite of the care with which Azuela organized the revised version of his novel, he sought to give the reader an initial impression that the work was somewhat disjointed. A simple reason for this may be that he realized that *Los de abajo* might well be published in the form of a newspaper serial. This would explain why the episodes are all of approximately equal length as well as why so many of them end on a climax and are virtually self-contained.[8] However, there are other explanations for this ambiguous structure. Azuela believed that new ideas, or new experiences, required new forms of expression (5, III, p.1122), and it is quite possible that he thought that an episodic structure, which was different from the flowing narrative of most nineteenth-century novels, was best suited to capturing the fragmentary nature of a revolution which evolved unpredictably and unguided by any dominant ideology. He thus wrote a series of representative cameos which would be seen only on careful examination to be linked, and the effect of which would be cumulative. An episodic structure has the virtue of presenting an impressionistic picture of the Revolution; this picture persuades the reader, by means other than logical argument, to reach the same pessimistic conclusions about the Revolution and the Mexican race as did Solís, and it does so by an identical process: that of providing apparently unconnected pieces of evidence which eventually come together to present the reader with an inescapable conclusion, a process described by Solís in Chapter 18 of Part I (quoted above on pp.37-38). Another explanation for the novel's structure is that Azuela may have wished to reproduce the common revolutionary's view of events of a chaotic war. This results in a structure which reflects the 'desorientación vesánica' (5, III, p.1266) which an isolated band of guerrillas must feel in any war, and particularly in one as complex and disparate as the Mexican Revolution. Furthermore, the apparent fragmentation of the structure might well reflect how the Revolution was experienced by peasants who did not relate one event to another discursively. A further explanation for Azuela's choice of structure is again a passage to be found in Part I, Chapter 18. Macías and his band have reached Fresnillo just before the attack on Zacatecas and there they have met

---

[8]Although Azuela may have had serialization in mind when he wrote *Los de abajo* and although it was first published in instalments, the type-setters of *El Paso del Norte* split the novel into *folletines* to suit their own convenience and with no regard to the author's chapter divisions. The instalments of the 1915 version frequently break off in mid-sentence and, on occasion, even in the middle of a word (*28*, pp.121-22).

Solís. He proceeds to recount to Macías the latter's own heroic military exploits:

> Alberto Solís, con fácil palabra y acento de sinceridad profunda, lo felicitó efusivamente por sus hechos de armas, por sus aventuras, que lo habían hecho famoso, siendo conocidas hasta por los mismos hombres de la poderosa División del Norte.

> Y Demetrio, encantado, oía el relato de sus hazañas, compuestas y aderezadas de tal suerte, que él mismo no las conociera. Por lo demás, aquello tan bien sonaba a sus oídos, que acabó por contarlas más tarde en el mismo tono y aun por creer que así habíanse realizado. (126)

Azuela may implicitly be making an important comment on his narrative: just as Cervantes had previously attributed to Macías motives for joining the Revolution which Macías never dreamed of (108-09), here another intellectual, Solís, acting as writer or story-teller, orders and embellishes events, distorting them beyond all recognition even for those who have been their protagonists. Yet this version is the one which the listener wants to hear far more than he wants the truth, Azuela's ironic style at this point clearly indicating his opinion of the sham with which Macías is being regaled. Azuela here anticipates how official Mexican historians would, like Solís, order, embellish, and simplify the events of the Revolution and, in so doing, would convert them into empty myths (Azuela later in the novel, 131, caricatures the way in which the popular legend of Villa distorts the truth). We must be cautious in attributing such an underlying meaning to this passage, for it is one of the more tiresome reflexes of modern literary critics to ferret out in all imaginative works passages which appear, or can somehow be made to appear, to be commenting on the process of narration itself. However, if it is not inappropriate to see Solís's rewriting of events as a comment upon the way narrative can falsify the truth, then Azuela may here be reassuring his readers that in his novel he cannot be accused of giving a neatly structured but false version of the Revolution. He thus preserves the illusion of the unembellished, truthful slice of life; yet, in order to convey a coherent message in an esthetically satisfying manner, he orders and structures his novel — albeit surreptitiously — in the ways I have suggested. Whether or not Azuela intended it, this passage can even be construed as a warning against those Procrustean critics who were to stretch and prune history to fit their preconceptions, and then judge his novels about the Revolution accordingly. As we have seen, *Los de abajo* has often been censured by those who would have us believe that Azuela's portrayal of brutality, sadism and thuggery is to be attributed more to a bewildered bourgeois's inadequate class analysis of the Revolution than to the fact that for most Mexicans the Revolution was, perhaps, just like the picture he paints of it. Such critics tend to suggest that the revealing of the author's latent ideology is the main interest in the novel and imply that Azuela's major shortcoming was his failure to share their own interpretation of the Revolution in particular and of the mechanisms of history in general.

   Los de abajo is a novel which is consciously though covertly structured by its author. Far from being merely the 'serie de cuadros y escenas de la revolución constitucionalista, débilmente atado por un hilo novelesco' or even the 'cuadros y escenas de la revolución actual' of Azuela's original subtitle, it is ordered and directed towards a particular goal, that of communicating a thesis about the corruption and failure of the Revolution, and of doing so in a manner which is both persuasive and palatable. Azuela's use of an expressive structure is an important and strikingly modern feature of *Los de abajo*. Some of the novel's other achievements will be examined in the Conclusion of this study.

5. Conclusion

Los de abajo distilled for Mexican readers the anarchic atmosphere of their Revolution, passed a moral judgement upon it, and provided an innovative literary model for the treatment of the Revolution in the many novels which were subsequently written. It still exerts considerable influence on modern Mexican novelists.

It is a short work in which Azuela maintains a striking dynamism by the use of concision in plot, narrative, dialogue, description, characterization and, more generally, prose style *(32, pp.124-25)*. As we have seen, the novel appears fragmentary, there is no digression or introduction of sub-plots, and the reader is merely given a sketch of what is happening and has to imagine or infer events at which the author only hints. These are some of the ways in which *Los de abajo* breaks with the tradition of nineteenth-century European novels.

The action begins dramatically *in medias res* and only gradually do we piece together some of the oblique references to what had taken place before the novel began. In a similar way, a turning-point in the history of the Revolution, the Aguascalientes Convention, is relegated to the gap between two Parts (indeed, this gap covers some six months' activity), while less important actions occur between chapters: at the end of Chapter 17 of the first Part Demetrio has some 20 comrades; by the beginning of Chapter 18, not only has his column increased to 100 men but Natera implies that, between the events described in these two chapters, Macías must have campaigned in several of the western provinces of Mexico and possibly taken part in the capture of Tepic in May 1914 (unless he means that Macías had been harassing *federales* even before the events recounted at the beginning of the novel; 124). We are given no further information about these campaigns; rather, we are left with the impression, as so often in the novel, that a wide-ranging Revolution is taking place but that we, like the characters, glimpse mere fragments or just hear rumours of it. Yet the impressionistic method Azuela employs builds up a picture of the Revolution which is, in some ways, more telling than that provided by a minutely detailed historical work (*5*, III, p.1098). Events are narrated economically: the moving parting of Macías and his wife at the beginning of the novel is reduced to two succinct sentences: 'Salieron juntos; ella con el niño en los brazos. Ya a la puerta se apartaron en opuesta dirección' (76). The only reference to the outcome of a clash between a hundred Catholic irregulars and Macías's band is a single graphic sentence describing the scene after the skirmish: 'El cura se quedaba allí bamboleándose, pendiente de un mezquite, y en el campo, un reguero de muertos que ostentaban en el pecho un escudito de bayeta roja y un letrero: "¡Detente! ¡El Sagrado Corazón de Jesús está conmigo!"' (161). This sentence is an example of Azuela's extreme compression of narration and description and, indeed, is a modification of the longer account of this action contained in the 1915 version of the novel. It conveys the mercilessness of the massacre, the word 'reguero' suggesting that the enemy were cut down as they fled (indeed, the original version described their scattering and being hunted down for fun like quails); the ingenuous faith of the victims makes their slaughter more barbaric; the silence regarding prisoners is ominous, for it implies that no quarter was given; the swaying corpse of the hanged priest is not only a horrific image which would become a cliché of Mexican films dealing with the Revolution, but implies the ruthlessness of the band; and the fact that it is a priest who has been executed, as well as a later reference to the plundering of the nearby church, is a clear reflection of the anti-clericalism which was a particular feature of the period during which *Los de abajo* is set (such anti-clericalism was a strong current among the revolutionaries yet coexisted with the superstitious faith we see in Macías and his band; *32*, pp.288-92). By leaving the details of the killing to our imagination, Azuela makes the scene particularly chilling, and even the laconic style of the single sentence is eloquent, for it mirrors both the revolutionaries' indifference to killing and Macías's scorn for an enemy who does not put up a decent fight.

Not only is the narrative compressed, but apparently insignificant details carry a charge of meaning, particularly for a contemporary Mexican reader who would have instantly understood the implications. In the first chapter, for example, the fact that the Federal officer is drunk would have suggested that the novel was here dealing with the period of Huerta's rule (something that is later confirmed), for Huerta's predilection for strong liquor was notorious and he was frequently caricatured by his enemies as a drunkard. In Chapter 2 of Part II, the brief exchange in a looted mansion between Pancracio and an unnamed individual who buys valuable plundered books from him at a ridiculously low price appears casual, but a contemporary reader would have seen it as an allusion to the way in which ordinary civilians took advantage of the Revolution and joined the scramble for easy money (143; see also 153-54, 179). Azuela implies that such people were even more despicable than the Revolutionaries, for, rather than risking their lives, they merely profited from the ignorance and fecklessness of the fighters. The brief description of Pancracio's anger in the same house,

> Pancracio manifestó su enojo de no encontrar algo que le
> complaciera, lanzando al aire con la punta del guarache
> un retrato encuadrado, cuyo cristal se estrelló en el
> candelabro del centro. (141)

not only provides a vivid impression of the opulence of the mansion, which is nowhere described by the narrator, but also the contrast between such luxury and Pancracio's 'guarache' speaks volumes about the gap between Mexico's rich and poor. All of this is achieved with remarkable concision (*29*, pp.82-89). These appear at first to be minor details but, like Solís's 'insignificancias', they build up the picture of the Revolution's 'mueca pavorosa' (see above, p.37). Azuela trusts his readers to pick up these passing references and, generally, does not insert digressive sermons in which he lectures us — a procedure to which he was, in theory, opposed (*5*, III, p.906).

Much of the novel consists of dialogue, and it should not surprise us that Azuela later maintained that the stage version of *Los de abajo* practically wrote itself. This dialogue has the effect of heightening the drama, bringing characters to life and implying much in a concise manner without the narrator's intervention, thus creating a semblance of authorial objectivity. From the very first chapter, the voices are recognizably Mexican in pronunciation, vocabulary and tone. As a realist writer, Azuela generally avoids the *costumbrismo* of his predecessors in his depiction of Mexican reality and does not draw attention in an exaggerated manner to his characters' regional Spanish. His long acquaintance with the country people of Jalisco had taught him how they talked (5, III, p.1057), and he reproduces convincingly the patterns and cadences of their speech. The narrative voice is also Mexican and colloquial; this is another way in which Azuela innovated in *Los de abajo*, moving away from European models to forge a narrative suited to the description of Mexican experience. Nevertheless, he does, on occasion, distance himself from popular language by enclosing within inverted commas colloquial expressions embedded in the narrative (e.g. 104, 127). His sensitivity to the spoken word enables him to use dialogue in several ways for the purpose of concision. Firstly, characters are distinguishable by their particular stylistic idiosyncrasies (see above pp.73-74) and there is frequently no need to interrupt the dialogue with phrases identifying the speakers. Secondly, his dialogue economically reveals the character of the speakers and their motives as well as referring obliquely to events, it being assumed that the reader is sensitive to nuances and silences and will pick up these implications. For example, the following exchanges:

— [Cervantes] Se nos están agotando los fondos...

— [Macías] ¡Cómo!... ¿Cuarenta mil pesos en ocho días? [...]

— [Cervantes] ¿En qué quedamos, pues, Codorniz?

— [Codorniz] Ya le dije, curro: doscientos por el puro reló ...

— [Cervantes] No, yo te compro a bulto: relojes, anillos
y todas las alhajitas. ¿Cuánto? (166-67)

indicate how Cervantes manipulates his ignorant comrades, the
juxtaposition of the two conversations at the same time suggesting
that he is embezzling their funds to acquire booty. The suspicion of
Cervantes's dishonesty in financial matters is merely planted in the
reader's mind and nothing more is said about it. Thirdly, Azuela
frequently ends conversations with three dots reproducing everyday
speech patterns realistically, for most of our conversations do not
consist of well rounded statements but, rather, are interrupted by
other speakers, trail off into silence, or are drowned out by noise and
laughter (e.g. '— Sí; le diste cantáridas pa... Los gritos de protesta de
Venancio se ahogaron entre las carcajadas estrepitosas de los demás';
98). The reader thus has to supply the missing words. Azuela also
uses this technique to solve the problem of mirroring in a realist
fashion the speech of people who would have larded their conversation with obscenities, and yet of doing so in language which would
be publishable. He thus suppresses the swearing while giving the
reader a clear indication of what was going to be said: 'Pa mí el tal
curro no es más que un...' (158); 'ellos no son más que unos hijos
de...' (172); '¡No nace todavía el hijo de la... que tenga que derrotar a
mi general Villa!' (186). On occasion he takes this much further and
develops a technique in which we hear only one side of a dialogue
and have to supply the other side ourselves. For example, in Chapter
9 of Part I, Camila quizzes Cervantes about the way he dresses his
wound (93-94). Not only do her questions reveal her naïve curiosity,
but the suppression of Cervantes's responses is an economical way of
conveying his indifference to her: his answers are so off-hand that
they are not even recorded.

Azuela despised verbose, flowery prose, believing that a self-
conscious style falsified reality and, by drawing attention to the
author's presence, shattered the illusion of truth to life after which
the realist writer strove. He claimed to have attempted, at least in his
early works, to write clearly and concisely and to have avoided using
high-flown literary language (5, III, p.1114), reproducing instead the

Mexican Spanish of everyday speech — something which led to his being accused by some Mexican critics of making grammatical mistakes in *Los de abajo* (Spanish critics, paradoxically, did not criticize his language: *31*, p.51). The style of *Los de abajo* is, indeed, remarkably spare and elliptical, with its short sentences, paragraphs and chapters, but he certainly polished it for the revised version, producing carefully-worked passages of description (compare, for example, the first paragraph of Part II, Chapter 9 with the original version (*28*, p.157; see also *26*, pp.155-57)). His style is, however, artfully simple, robust, laconic and almost staccato; it serves as an effective medium for his narration of common people's involvement in brutal events, suggests much more than it states, and contrasts with the highly mannered *modernista* mode which was in vogue among his contemporaries in Spanish America. Indeed,. one of the few reviews the book received when it appeared in 1915 talks of its 'estilo conciso, sencillo y claro' and its 'lenguaje castizo de "los de abajo"' (*28*, p.96). When Azuela uses a high-flown style it is frequently to mock the pseudo-revolutionary rhetoric of characters like Cervantes. His acute ear produces fine parody, such overwrought language being used to ridicule the speaker or the sentiments expressed and often being deflated by events or other characters (87, 92-93, 108-09, 119-20, 124). Elsewhere, elaborate prose draws attention to itself for an ironic purpose. Thus he added to the 1920 version a paragraph which, with its poetic cadences, recherché vocabulary, alliteration and *esdrújula* stresses, is deliberately beautiful, yet describes how two fighting cocks tear each other to pieces for the amusement of the soldiers, suggesting a clear parallel with the Revolution itself:

> Como movidos por un resorte, los gallos se lanzaron al encuentro. Sus cuellos crespos y encorvados, los ojos como corales, erectas las crestas, crispadas las patas, un instante se mantuvieron sin tocar el suelo siquiera, confundidos sus plumajes, picos y garras en uno solo; el retinto se desprendió y fue lanzado patas arriba más allá de la raya. Sus ojos de cinabrio se apagaron, cerráronse

lentamente sus párpados coriáceos, y sus plumas
esponjadas se estremecieron convulsas en un charco de
sangre. (188)

Azuela frequently has recourse to imagery, and the care with which
it is employed increases its impact. Functional imagery precludes the
need for authorial comment and, by suggesting much in a short
space, contributes to the overall impression of concision given by the
novel. Thus La Bufa at Zacatecas is likened to the 'testa
empenachada de altivo rey azteca' (133), implying, through the
suggestion of Aztec sacrificial ceremonies, an inherent Mexican
bloodlust going beyond this particular battle (which was one of the
most bloody of the war). It is consequently foreboding when we
encounter a parallel image in the final Part of the novel (183).
Azuela's pessimistic view of the Revolution, even at the high point
of the victory at Zacatecas, is encapsulated in a prophetic symbol
which immediately precedes Solís's death. As Solís surveys the
battlefield,

> Su sonrisa volvió a vagar siguiendo las espirales de
> humo de los rifles y la polvareda de cada casa derribada
> y cada techo que se hundía. Y creyó haber descubierto
> un símbolo de la revolución en aquellas nubes de humo
> y en aquellas nubes de polvo que fraternalmente
> ascendían, se abrazaban, se confundían y se borraban en
> la nada. (135)

The revolutionary forces have united in the common struggle to
defeat the evils of the Federación, but this spirit of co-operation to
achieve a positive goal is as ephemeral as clouds of smoke.
Moreover, it is ominous that such clouds representing the revolutionaries are the product of gunfire and destruction. Similarly,
Azuela will symbolize the Revolution in a passing reference or
allusion. A typewriter, standing for culture, order and civilization, is
dashed against some rocks by an illiterate guerrilla (127-28). At the
end of the 1920 version, the revolutionaries appear as cripples and

consumptives (190) — an accurate reference to the large number of wounded soldiers who were the legacy of the Revolution and to the diseases which ravaged Mexico as *villismo* declined, but also a fitting metaphor for men whom the Revolution left 'mutilados del espíritu' (5, III, p.1267), doomed and exhausted, yet still infecting all around them.

Concision is also achieved by Azuela's pervasive irony which substitutes implication for explanation; thus the bestial cockfight referred to above is described as being 'de una ferocidad casi humana' (188). Similarly, Cervantes carries out with 'rara solicitud' the order to burn down Don Mónico's house (154), but it is implied on the next page that his eagerness to obey Macías's command was really a desire for the money he was able to extort from Don Mónico, doubtless through some compromise with that representative of the *caciques* he affects to despise. Solís sincerely narrates his loss of ideals to a man whom he believes to cherish an idealistic view of the Revolution, while the reader is aware that the real idealist was bound to become disillusioned by what he saw around him and that it was only the hypocrite who had never entertained a positive view of the Revolution who could pretend to remain an idealist (125-26). Likewise, Macías and Anastasio Montañés envy Cervantes's learning, believing that it enables him to understand the Revolution, while we know that this understanding will be used only to exploit the likes of Macías and Anastasio (109). As is the case with the novel's overall circularity, which suggests the Revolution's failure to achieve anything worthwhile, Azuela employs irony to pass concise, bitter yet implicit judgements. It is also used to build up considerable tension towards the end of the novel: when the narrator states of Macías's band as they head towards the ambush in which they will be wiped out, 'Nadie piensa en la artera bala que puede estarlo esperando más adelante' (195), we realize what awaits them and, as so often in this novel in which the inexorability of events is stressed, the tension leads less to surprise than to the fulfilment of our expectations.

For all its concision, it would be wrong to claim that *Los de abajo* is a perfectly crafted work, and its author would certainly never have done so. I have drawn attention to its considerable subtleties, to its structure which is less arbitrary than has often been assumed, and to the vividness of some, at least, of its character-portrayal. Nevertheless, it remains a work the first version of which was improvised and even when revised is still somewhat rough and ready. There are, for example, several instances when Azuela makes mistakes of chronology. One such example is his muddle about the time covered by the events of the novel. Shortly before the battle of Zacatecas, which took place in June 1914, Cervantes claims to have been a revolutionary for two months (125); on returning to Juchipila, Macías's band remember that Zacatecas had fallen to them one year previously (192); in the next chapter Azuela tells us that Macías and his wife had not seen each other for almost two years (193), that is since mid or late 1913. This would mean that almost ten months had elapsed either between Macías's leaving his wife and Cervantes's joining the band, or between Macías's return to Juchipila and his conversation with his wife. Other passages show that neither explanation is true.[9] A different kind of oversight occurs when, near the end of the novel, Macías reminds Anastasio of 'aquel peón de Tepatitlán' (191) whom he had met in Part II (163-65), but neither was Anastasio present at that encounter nor could it have taken place in Tepatitlán, for the day after the meeting Macías had set off for that town. Of course, Macías could just have been confused himself, but it appears more likely that Azuela had forgotten the details contained in the earlier chapters of his novel.

The letter which introduces the final Part has frequently been criticized as a clumsy device for providing much undramatized information rapidly and for implausibly killing off three superfluous characters. Yet Azuela has been careful to suggest elsewhere in the

---

[9]Many critics, basing themselves on the reference to Demetrio's two-year absence from his wife, date the beginning of the events depicted in the novel to mid or late 1913. This is not, however, consistent with Cervantes's statement, and there is no reason why even a liar like Cervantes should have claimed to have been a revolutionary for many months fewer than he had. I have found no way of reconciling these and other contradictory indications about the date of some of the novel's events.

novel that Pancracio and El Manteca frequently become violent when playing cards, and so it is not entirely incredible that they should have killed each other in a brawl; Margarito has similarly been portrayed as an unstable character, and suicide is not an implausible end for him; and Cervantes's writing from the safety of the United States to inform those whom he exploited of his good fortune and to flatter Venancio into parting with his loot is entirely in character. However, it is the heavy-handed irony of the letter, with the ludicrous suggestion that Venancio join the Salvation Army, that makes it unbelievable. Azuela here offends against the realism of much of the rest of the novel by making Cervantes not just cynical but exaggeratedly so.

Indeed, Azuela's irony can sometimes be so exaggerated that it degenerates into sarcasm. The 1920 version is considerably more bitter than that of 1915, reflecting the author's increased disillusion bred by the duplicity of the revolutionary leaders and the development of the Revolution in the intervening years. Although Azuela had already mocked the ignorance and uncouthness of the mass of the revolutionaries (e.g. 86, 140-41, 145-46, 160, 180), in 1920 he is more caustic in his portrayal of them: thus, for example, the large number of self-styled generals among the revolutionary forces is satirized in the change from the original '¡Oh: es lástima que ese señor decente no esté por ahí para fusilarlo cada cinco minutos siquiera!' (*28*, p.163) to the later '¡Oh, es lástima que ese señor decente no esté a la mano para que lo fusilen siquiera cada uno de los generales que van allí!' (177-78). Similarly, the stupidity of the troops is pilloried when their general agreement that robbery is outrageous while murder is perfectly justifiable, is altered from 'Todos convienen' (*28*, p.163) to 'Todos parecen asentir ante tan graves razones' (178). Azuela's indignant voice is heard clearly here, as it is when he talks of 'la traición al presidente Madero' (119) or the 'Advenedizos de banqueta' (190). Such intervention jars with the illusion he creates elsewhere in the novel that events narrate themselves, the reader being left to draw his own conclusions from the actions and words of the characters. The ethical on occasion gets the better of the esthetic just as it does when characters seem to

mouth the author's own sentiments rather than having an inner life of
their own, in spite of Azuela's own theoretical objections to such a
procedure (e.g. 125-26, 135; see also *32*, pp.90-91). Likewise, some
of the natural descriptions written in an almost *modernista* poetic
prose, especially those associated with Camila, with whom Nature is
made to sympathize (112), sit uneasily with the deliberately simple
style adopted by Azuela in the rest of the novel.

Some of these criticisms may well be pedantic. Azuela claims
to have been unconcerned with and unimpressed by professional
critics, and he saw himself as a straightforward man writing for a
popular Mexican readership (*5*, III, p.1118) about the common
experience of his countrymen during their Revolution. His achievements and innovations in *Los de abajo* are considerable, especially
when the literary background against which he was writing in
Mexico is considered, and his novel has captured the imagination of
generations of Mexican and foreign readers to become the most
famous work of the sub-genre normally referred to as the novel of
the Mexican Revolution. *Los de abajo* was the product of immediate
experience and set out to portray a particular reality, the 1915
version being promoted by a contemporary advertisement as 'el
trasunto más fiel de la contienda civil en México. Su autor no adula a
ninguno de los partidos políticos y con la verdad desnuda dolorosa-
mente flagela el crimen y la injusticia en donde quiera que lo
encuentra, sin restricciones ni piedad alguna' (*28*, p.93). It is some
measure of the success of his tense and terse narrative and his bleak
vision of those particular events, with the brutality, casual violence,
misery and waste of human life they entailed, that for many readers
this short and unpretentious work has taken on a much wider significance. In terms of literary history it has come to be seen as a
landmark in the development of Latin-American narrative, drawing
as it did upon the traditions of nineteenth-century European fiction
and yet adapting and developing them in an original fashion to
portray a uniquely Latin-American experience.

Bibliographical Note

Of the many articles, chapters and books which discuss *Los de abajo* I have
included only those which either have made a significant contribution to my
appreciation of the novel or which represent approaches frequently encountered in criticism of Azuela's work. The country or place of publication of
journals is provided in parentheses where confusion may occur.

A. BIBLIOGRAPHIES

1. David William Foster, *Mexican Literature: A Bibliography of
   Secondary Sources* (Metuchen, NJ: Scarecrow Press, 1981), pp.95-
   105.
2. John Rutherford, *An Annotated Bibliography of the Novels of the
   Mexican Revolution of 1910-1917 in English and Spanish* (Troy, NY:
   Whitston Publishing Co., 1972), pp.33-39.

B. AZUELA'S WORKS

3. Mariano Azuela, *Los de abajo*, ed. W.A.R. Richardson (London:
   Harrap, 1973 and subsequent reprints). Contains a full introduction and
   useful explanatory and linguistic notes to the text.
4. ——, *Los de abajo*, ed. Jorge Ruffinelli, Colección Archivos, 5
   (Madrid: UNESCO, 1988). An excellent critical edition of the text
   accompanied by a series of essays, several of a high standard; three are
   versions of the items listed below as *22, 28,* and *31*. Also contains
   Azuela's comments on *Los de abajo* and a good bibliography.
5. ——, *Obras completas*, 3 vols (Mexico City: Fondo de Cultura
   Económica, 1958-60).
6. ——, *Epistolario y archivo*, ed. Beatrice Berler, Nueva Biblioteca
   Mexicana, 11 (Mexico City: Centro de Estudios Literarios, Universidad
   Nacional Autónoma de México, 1969).

C. HISTORICAL BACKGROUND

7. Alan Knight, *The Mexican Revolution*, 2 vols (Cambridge: UP, 1986; repr. Lincoln, NE: Univ. of Nebraska Press, 1990). A splendid book which, although meticulously detailed, is readable and well indexed.
8. John Womack Jr., 'The Mexican Revolution, 1910-1920', in *The Cambridge History of Latin America*, ed. Leslie Bethell, V (Cambridge: UP, 1986), pp.79-153. A briefer account than Knight's, written by another leading historian of the Revolution.

(*3* and *32* both contain brief accounts of the Revolution)

D. CRITICAL STUDIES

9. Diarmuid Bradley, 'Aspects of Realism in Azuela's *Los de abajo*', *Ibero-Amerikanisches Archiv*, 4 (1978), 39-55. Useful article on Azuela's realist theory and practice, also containing several acute observations on *Los de abajo*.
10. ———, 'The Thematic Import of Azuela's *Los de abajo*: A Defence', *Forum for Modern Language Studies*, 15 (1979), 14-25. Maintains that the novel is a tragedy but not deterministic, the characters being allowed to exercise moral freedom.
11. John S. Brushwood, *Mexico in its Novel: A Nation's Search for Identity* (Austin: Univ. of Texas Press, 1966); Spanish translation: *México en su novela* (Mexico City: Fondo de Cultura Económica, 1973). One of several general surveys of the development of the modern Mexican novel. In particular (pp.178-81 of the English original) draws attention to the ambiguities of *Los de abajo*.
12. Adalbert Dessau, *La novela de la Revolución mexicana*, Colección Popular, 117 (Mexico City: Fondo de Cultura Económica, 1972). Well documented; discusses Azuela's works at some length. Based on a Marxist analysis of the Revolution, this study claims that Azuela's portrayal of events was not only partial but also inaccurate and that his failure to perceive the Revolution as a class struggle was responsible for the artistic shortcomings of *Los de abajo*. (Extract in *30*.)
13. Víctor Díaz Arciniega, 'Retórica y refrito', *Revista de la Universidad de México*, 38 = new series, 19 (1982), 40-44. Incisive critique of the simplistic political interpretations (and, implicitly, condemnations) of Azuela's works which have been popular among some critics.
14. ———, 'Mariano Azuela y *Los de abajo*: entre "ser" y "representar"', *Investigación Humanística* (Mexico City), 3 (1987), 117-41. Examines the way in which Azuela's novel has been institutionalized in Mexico and employed by critics to serve their own ideological ends.

15. John E. Englekirk, 'The "Discovery" of *Los de abajo*', *Hispania* (U.S.A.), 18 (1935), 53-62. Provides a useful account of the debate which surrounded the recognition of the novel's importance by Mexican critics in 1924 and 1925 and which led to its fame. (Also in *30*.)

16. Sergio Fernández, *Retratos del fuego y la ceniza*, Letras Mexicanas, 91 (Mexico City: Fondo de Cultura Económica, 1968), pp.81-93. On Camila and La Pintada. Unfocused, but contains several helpful insights, especially into the character of the latter.

17. Dick Gerdes, 'Point of View in *Los de abajo*', *Hispania* (U.S.A.), 64 (1981), 557-63. Identifies narrative techniques which contribute to the apparent objectivity and dramatic power of the novel.

18. Luis Leal, *Mariano Azuela: vida y obra*, Colección Studium, 30 (Mexico City: Ediciones de Andrea, 1961). This book and *19* are the only serious attempts to study Azuela's output as a whole. They are simple in their approach and contain useful information.

19. ———, *Mariano Azuela*, Twayne's World Authors Series, 119 (New York: Twayne, 1971). See comments on *18*.

20. Carlos R. Luis, '*Los de abajo*, narración crítica', *Filología* (Buenos Aires), 15 (1979), 125-33. Maintains that the use of perspectivism and a certain absence of an omniscient narrator leads to the impression of objectivity and a reflection of the complexity of the Revolution.

21. Gerald Martin, 'Mariano Azuela's Point of View in *Los de abajo*', *Vida Hispánica: Journal of the Association of Teachers of Spanish and Portuguese*, 32, no. 2 (Autumn 1983), 39-46. Representative of a study of the novel from a left-wing viewpoint; contains several helpful observations.

22. Seymour Menton, 'La estructura épica de *Los de abajo* y un prólogo especulativo', *Hispania* (U.S.A.), 50 (1967), 1001-11. Argues for an ordered structure to the novel and contains many helpful insights; the central thesis that the structure of the novel is somehow epic is, nevertheless, unconvincing. (This influential article is reworked in *4*, pp.239-50.)

23. Francisco Monterde (ed.), *Mariano Azuela y la crítica mexicana*, SepSetentas, 86 (Mexico City: Secretaría de Educación Pública, 1973). Anthology of writing about Azuela's works; much of it ephemeral, but includes some of the earliest criticism of *Los de abajo*.

24. Timothy Murad, 'Animal Imagery and Structural Unity in Mariano Azuela's *Los de abajo*', *Journal of Spanish Studies: Twentieth Century*, 7 (1979), 207-22. Contains several useful observations.

25. ———, 'Foreshadowing, Duplication, and Structural Unity in Mariano Azuela's *Los de abajo*', *Hispania* (U.S.A.), 64 (1981), 550-56. Provides examples of internal parallelism to argue for a coherent structure to the novel.

26. Enrique Pupo-Walker, 'El protagonista en la evolución textual de *Los de abajo*', in *Estudios de literatura hispanoamericana en honor a José J. Arrom*, ed. Andrew P. Debicki and Enrique Pupo-Walker, North Carolina Studies in the Romance Languages and Literatures, Symposia, 2 (Chapel Hill: Department of Romance Languages, Univ. of North Carolina, 1974), pp.155-66. Suggestive study of the development of Demetrio's character in the light of revisions made by Azuela for the 1920 edition.

27. Angel Rama, 'Mariano Azuela: ambición y frustración de las clases medias', in his *Literatura y clase social* (Mexico City: Folios Ediciones, 1984), pp.144-83 [this essay was first published under the title 'El perspectivismo social en la novela de Mariano Azuela', *Revista Iberoamericana de Literatura* (Montevideo), 1 (1966), 63-94]. Claims that Azuela's depiction of the Revolution is determined by the political beliefs and experiences of the middle classes of which he is said to be a representative. Despite Rama's facile ideological approach, he makes several helpful comments concerning Azuela's view of the role played by Mexican intellectuals in the Revolution.

28. Stanley L. Robe, *Azuela and the Mexican Underdogs*, UCLA Latin American Studies Series, 48 (Berkeley: Univ. of California Press, 1979). Reproduces the text of the original 1915 version published as a newspaper serial in El Paso (with the exception of two instalments which have disappeared); also contains a well-researched introduction to the novel. (A shorter version of this introduction is to be found in *4*, pp.153-84.)

29. Hugo Rodríguez-Alcalá, 'Mariano Azuela y las antítesis de *Los de abajo*', in his *Ensayos de norte a sur*, Colección Studium, 27 (Mexico City: Ediciones de Andrea; Seattle: Univ. of Washington Press, 1960), pp.81-91. Illustrates the concision of Azuela's narrative.

30. Rogelio Rodríguez Coronel (ed.), *Recopilación de textos sobre la novela de la Revolución mexicana* (Havana: Casa de las Américas, 1975). Useful anthology of excerpts from critical articles and books about the novels of the Mexican Revolution, including *Los de abajo*.

31. Jorge Ruffinelli, '*Los de abajo* y sus contemporáneos: Mariano Azuela y los límites del liberalismo', *Literatura Mexicana* (Mexico City), 1 (1990), 41-64. Traces the history of the novel's reception in Mexico and abroad, the official glorification of Azuela as a national figure, and the place of *Los de abajo* in the polemic about the Revolution's achievements. (This article is a reworking of *4*, pp.185-213.)

32. John Rutherford, *Mexican Society during the Revolution: A Literary Approach* (Oxford: Clarendon, 1971). Revised Spanish translation: *La sociedad mexicana durante la Revolución*, Colección Fragua Mexicana, 24 (Mexico City: Ediciones El Caballito, 1978). The best book about the novels of the Revolution; discusses the portrayal in literary works

of the antagonists of the Revolution, and of contemporary Mexican institutions; contains substantial sections on Azuela's works. References are to the English original.

33. Porfirio Sánchez, 'La deshumanización del hombre en *Los de abajo*', *Cuadernos Americanos*, 33 (1974), 179-91. Some helpful comments about the characters.

34. Richard Young, 'Narrative Structure in Two Novels by Mariano Azuela: *Los caciques* and *Los de abajo*', *Revista Canadiense de Estudios Hispánicos*, 2 (1977-78), 169-81. Argues that, while these two novels have episodic structures, such structures are not arbitrary but, rather, were devised to embody a particular interpretation of the Revolution.

CRITICAL GUIDES TO SPANISH TEXTS

Edited by
J.E. Varey, A.D. Deyermond and C. Davies

CRITICAL GUIDES TO SPANISH TEXTS

Edited by
J.E. Varey, A.D. Deyermond and C. Davies